EIGHT WEEKS TO

Collaborative

CO-PARENTING

FOR DIVORCING PARENTS

YOUR JOURNEY TO BECOMING A BETTER PARENT
AND PERSON DURING THE DIVORCE PROCESS

www.COLLABORATIVECOPARENTING.com

BY CAROL F. DELZER, M.A., J.D.

First edition copyright ©2009 Carol F. Delzer, M.A., J.D.

ISBN: 0-9824159-5-8
ISBN-13: 9780982415955

Published by Collaborative Co-Parenting, Sacramento, California

Visit www.Amazon.com to order additional copies.

To Art, my daughter's father, for his support through years of collaborative co-parenting and his willingness to let me tell our stories. Thank you.

And to Jessica for being such a cool and flexible kid who helped her mom and dad turn a difficult situation into a wonderful life for us all. Thank you for growing up to be such a beautiful person inside and out.

ACKNOWLEDGEMENTS

This book would not have been possible without the support and encouragement of the staff at my law firm, Family Law Center. Special thanks go to Jamie Miller, my law office manager, who keeps my law firm running smoothly so I have time to expand my creativity.

So many professionals have contributed to this book. I am grateful for the family law community, including lawyers, court mediators, and therapists, who contributed their time, efforts, and professional insights to this project. I am particularly grateful to Patricia Clark, an attorney at Family Law Center, for helping me to kick-start this book.

I would also like to thank Jane Nelsen, my longtime friend and co-author of *Positive Discipline for Single Parents*. Jane inspired me to write this book and encouraged me to finish it.

Other key people in the project were Diana Erwin and Candy Chand, my writers, and Ellen Levy, my diligent, articulate editor.

Finally, I would like to express my gratitude and love for my daughter, Jessica, who inspires me to be the best person I can be. She's not only an awesome kid, but also my best friend. Thank you, Jessica, for your contributions and design work on www.CollaborativeCoparenting.com.

TABLE OF CONTENTS

EXPANDED TABLE OF CONTENTS

Week 2: Building the Collaborative Co-Parenting Relationship

Week 3: Resolving Conflict

Week 4: Managing Emotions

Week 5: Appreciating Differences

Week 6: Parenting Tools

Week 7: Designing a Workable Parenting Plan

Week 8: Special Challenges

You Can Do It!

INTRODUCTION TO THE AUTHOR

Let me tell you a little bit about myself and why I wrote this easy-to-follow, 8-week course on co-parenting. I created the course for you, a person who wants to be the best parent possible for the sake of your children. I also wrote it because I've been where you are—a divorced single parent.

When my daughter Jessica was two years old, I found myself struggling with the decision to end my marriage while wondering how I would cope as a single mother. I was fearful and uncertain about my future.

I wanted to choose a career that would support my daughter and me financially. I also was determined to understand why my relationship failed and why relationships overall are so challenging.

Shortly after my divorce, I co-authored a book with my friend, Jane Nelsen, a nationally known speaker and expert on parenting and author of the *Positive Discipline* series. I realized in co-authoring this book that I had something unique and special to offer other divorcing and single parents. From this passion, I decided to open my family law mediation practice.

I went on to become a marriage-family therapist and found that these skills give me the ability to relate to parents in a more meaningful way. Because I am a therapist, clients are willing to let me into their private lives more than if I were just an attorney.

This combination allows me to help divorcing parents understand that people who work together to create agreements that are satisfactory to both are more likely to follow them and less likely to be angry, destructive, or hurtful.

Congratulations on taking an important step toward becoming the best parent possible during and after your divorce.

~ Carol Delzer, M.A., J.D.

HOW TO BENEFIT FROM
THIS 8-WEEK COURSE

This course's aim is to pass on the gift of a collaborative, committed co-parent relationship to you. In order to receive the benefits of this course, you need to do your part. Take the necessary time to read the book—one chapter a week—and do the Action Items each week which are listed at the end of each chapter.

This book can also be used in co-parenting groups, ideally led by a counselor or therapist. If that is not available, find other people who want to be better co-parents and work through the book as a group.

During your journey you may be pleasantly surprised to find that there are additional benefits as well. At the end of the 8 weeks, you will be more than a better parent—you'll also discover a more productive, peaceful, and happier you.

"Forget mistakes. Forget failure.
Forget everything except what
you're going to do now, and do it.
Today is your lucky day."
~ Will Durant, American historian

WEEK 1, BEGINNING YOUR JOURNEY

"The greatest gift you can give your children istwo parents who can work together collaboratively."
~ Carol Delzer, course author

What You Will Find in Week 1:

- The Importance of Collaborative Co-Parenting for Your Children
- Collaborative Co-Parenting Course Agreement
- Creating a New Life
- Letting Go of the Past
- The Nine Steps to Forgiveness
- Discovering What is Unique About Your Children
- Understanding Children's Emotions
- Voices of the Children

THE IMPORTANCE OF COLLABORATIVE CO-PARENTING FOR YOUR CHILDREN

The parent-child relationship is one of the most important, life-changing bonds you'll ever have. Making wise decisions regarding parenting is critical for you and your children.

I believe parents want the best for their children. Despite that, divorce and relationship breakups happen every day. The common stresses surrounding this life event can create enormous tension for the entire family. Sadly, children often become the innocent victims of a negative breakup experience.

But take heart—you can change that situation. I will show you how to make decisions and work with your co-parent in a more productive way.

During this 8-week course, you'll discover how to protect your children from the heartbreak, the chaos, and the expense that often make the divorce process traumatic. By learning how to avoid the mistakes of others, you'll gain fresh insight into how to support and nurture your children in the years ahead. You will give your children the chance to look back on these years as a happy period touched by divorce, rather than a childhood devastated by it.

What you will learn in this course is called "collaborative co-parenting." Collaborative co-parenting means finding a way to work with your co-parent with dignity and respect. It is more like a business relationship than a personal relationship. You collaborate with your co-parent, setting aside your personal feelings, for the benefit of your children. You do this because your children need both of you for guidance, love, and support.

If you feel the road you're on right now with your co-parent is rocky or you want to learn more ideas for collaborative co-parenting, then join us on a new path. Through this 8-week life course, you can leave fear and anger behind and move toward openness, wisdom, and effective co-parenting. You will move closer to becoming the person you want to be.

Ideally, both parents will take this course. If that is not possible and you are beginning this journey alone, I want to commend you. Your actions *will* make a difference in your children's lives. Perhaps your co-parent will one day follow your lead and take the course. Even if that doesn't happen, you and your children will benefit as you begin your new lives.

The Course Agreement

I understand that from where you are now, it may be difficult to see down the road. But trust that with work, patience, and determination, the path will unfold before you, making your journey to becoming a better parent, co-parent, and person clearer each step of the way.

At this time, we ask you to sign a co-parent commitment agreement. This commitment will support you as you do the necessary work in the weeks ahead. This course asks you for four things: commitment, patience, determination, and trust.

Collaborative Co-Parenting Course Agreement

- I (fill in your name) _____
  will commit to taking part in this 8-week co-parenting course and promise to take seriously the lessons, exercises, journaling, and action items so I can become the best co-parent possible.
- I will give it the time necessary for the sake of my child(ren) as well as my own personal growth. I am accountable to myself and to my commitment to this 8-week course.

- I will trust, be determined, committed and patient to receive the benefits this course has to offer.
- At the end of the 8-week course, I commit to re-evaluating how I've changed so I can chart my progress.
- I will have the option of taking a confidential review course and online test at www.CollaborativeCoparenting.com to earn a certificate of completion. This certificate will ask me to sign a statement verifying that I completed the entire course.

Signature: _____

Date: _____

Suggestion: attach a photo of your
children to this page to remind
yourself why you're taking the course.

~ EXERCISE ~

What Do You Want to Gain from This Course?
Make a list of what you want to gain during this 8-week course.

_____

_____

_____

_____

Creating a New Life
Life is full of change. Sometimes it's welcome, but other times it's terrifying. Getting divorced and becoming a single parent are rarely welcome changes. The physical, emotional, and financial adjustments can be overwhelming. Right now, your life may seem broken beyond repair. It may be hard to believe, but this can be a positive time in your life. If you are willing to make changes and let go of the past, you have the opportunity to create a rewarding new life for yourself and your children. This course can help you do that. Remember that it takes change to make change. Focus on changing yourself rather than trying

> **"Letting Go" Affirmations**
>
> *I am letting go of resentment.*
> *I am letting go of anger.*
> *I am letting go of humiliation.*
> *I am letting go of fear.*
> *I am letting go of disappointment.*
> *I am letting go of past conflicts.*
> *I am letting go of emotional wounds.*
> *I am letting go of blame.*
> *I am letting go of lashing out.*
> *I am letting go of what might have been.*
> *I am letting go of the past.*

to change your co-parent. As you implement positive changes, your co-parent may become more willing to change as well.

The weeks and months ahead will be challenging. To transition from being intimate partners to parenting partners, you must stop blaming, stop indulging in negative thinking, and stop dwelling on the past. You will need to rebuild trust with your co-parent, learn to resolve conflict, and improve your communication skills. All of this will be easier if you remember that you're doing it for your children—and for yourself too.

Divorce is a painful experience for everyone involved, but it is also an opportunity for change. If you can learn to work with your co-parent despite your differences, you will have taken the first step toward building a rewarding new life.

Letting Go of the Past

As you move into this journey—letting go of the past and moving forward—it's important to put yourself in a positive frame of mind. Make sure you aren't letting your feelings about the past undermine the good work you're about to do during these 8 weeks.

Letting go of the past with all its hurt, resentment, anger, humiliation, and disappointment is important because holding onto those feelings keeps you from healing and moving forward. Your children need a healthy, supportive, loving "you" and a working partnership between their two parents. Letting go of the past will free you to be the best parent and person you can be.

Letting go of the past is not the same as simply telling yourself to "get over" your emotions. It does not mean that you should pretend your past relationship never happened or that you're not hurting when, in fact, you are.

What it *does* mean is learning to live each day in the present without constantly letting negative notions such as resentment, anger, and blame pull you down. It means being in the "now" and looking forward, not backward.

Letting go of the past also leaves you more open to setting goals, taking on new challenges, and facing an exciting (and sometimes scary) future. Talking to a therapist or counselor may help you let go of the past.

There will be more information on how to balance working through your emotions and letting go of the past in Week 4, the Managing Emotions chapter.

> *"When you forgive, you in no way change the past—but you sure do change the future."*
> ~ Bernard Meltzer, American radio host

The Nine Steps to Forgiveness

Forgiving your former spouse or yourself may seem impossible, but it's not. Forgiveness is actually something you do for yourself and your children. It will lighten the emotional burden you are carrying and make it easier to be a good parent and an effective co-parent.

Fred Luskin, Ph.D., is the director of the Stanford University Forgiveness Projects and the co-chair of the Garden of Forgiveness Project at Ground Zero in Manhattan. He shares the following advice for forgiving another person.

1. Know exactly how you feel about what happened and be able to articulate what about the situation is not OK. Then tell a trusted couple of people about your experience.

2. Make a commitment to yourself to do what you have to do to feel better. Forgiveness is for you and not for anyone else.

3. Forgiveness does not necessarily mean reconciliation with the person that hurt you or condoning their action. What you are after is to find peace. Forgiveness can be defined as the "peace and understanding that come from blaming that which has hurt you less, taking the life experience less personally, and changing your grievance story."

4. Get the right perspective on what is happening. Recognize that your primary distress is coming from the hurt feelings, thoughts, and physical upset you are suffering now, not what offended you or hurt you two minutes—or ten years—ago. Forgiveness helps to heal those hurt feelings.

5. At the moment you feel upset, practice a simple stress management technique to soothe your body's flight or fight response.

6. Give up expecting things from other people, or your life, that they do not choose to give you. Recognize the "unenforceable rules" you have for your health or how you or other people must behave. Remind yourself that you can hope for health, love, peace, and prosperity and work hard to get them.

7. Put your energy into looking for another way to get your positive goals met than through the experience that has hurt you. Instead of mentally replaying your hurt seek out new ways to get what you want.

8. Remember that a life well lived is your best revenge. Instead of focusing on your wounded feelings, and thereby giving the person who caused you pain power over you, learn to look for the love, beauty, and kindness around you. Forgiveness is about personal power.

9. Amend your grievance story to remind you of the heroic choice to forgive.

The practice of forgiveness has been shown to reduce anger, hurt, depression, and stress and leads to greater feelings of hope, peace, compassion, and self-confidence. Practicing forgiveness leads to healthy relationships as well as physical health. It also opens the heart to kindness, beauty, and love. For more information on forgiveness from Fred Luskin, visit the Resources section at collaborativeparenting.com.

~ EXERCISE ~

What Is Unique About My Child?
Your children are individuals with unique characteristics. Knowing what makes your children unique will help you stay focused on your priorities and provide the extra support they need. Please answer the questions below. If you have more than one child, fill out a line for each child.

What are some things that make my child happy?

_____

_____

_____

_____

_____

What are some of my child's strengths?

_____

_____

_____

_____

What is unique about my child?

_____

_____

_____

_____

When have I seen my child unhappy or upset during my divorce or relationship breakup?

_____

_____

_____

_____

Where might my child need extra help or support?

_____

_____

_____

_____

What can I do to give my child extra help and support?

_____

_____

_____

_____

By taking part in this exercise, you've gained greater awareness into your children's uniqueness and needs. This insight will help you as you move forward with this program and learn new co-parenting skills.

Understanding Children's Emotions

During your breakup, your children likely will have a lot of questions and concerns, expressed or not, such as:

- Who am I going to live with now?
- Is this my fault?
- Why do they keep arguing?
- Who gets to keep the house we live in?
- Why do they keep saying bad things about one another?
- What else will change?

Learning to respond to your children's feelings is valuable—to you and to them. Your children's questions and feelings give you important information about how they are coping and adjusting during the divorce process. Are your children displaying feelings of fear? Anxiety? Anger? Or perhaps they are hiding their feelings from you.

Understanding how to read your children's emotions is important, especially during a time of separation or breakup. Allowing your children to express their feelings sends a message of caring. It also builds trust so they can share other matters with you too.

Tips on How to Respond to Your Children's Feelings

- Ask your children to talk about what they are feeling.
- Listen to any feelings your children may be expressing, such as anger or revenge.
- Be a role model of how to deal with stress and anger in appropriate ways.
- If your children are having a hard time but don't feel comfortable talking to you about the divorce, arrange for them to talk to a neutral person, such as a therapist, child specialist, or a pastoral counselor.
- If your children get upset while talking, encourage them to take a cooling-off period during which they can calm down.
- Set aside time to just sit with your children quietly for reflection and discussion.
- For younger children, use art projects such as drawings as an opportunity for them to express themselves.

Voices of the Children

Knowing what children of divorce feel and worry about can help you make the best decisions for you and your children as you make changes in your life. Making changes that take your children's needs into account is only possible if you understand those needs. Listen to these children and see if their thoughts might echo the feelings of your children.

CHILDREN ON PARENTS FIGHTING

"Now that they've split up, I don't really understand why they're still fighting. They're like, 'You said this,' 'No, you said that.' Sometimes I just want to yell, 'Stop it! You're acting so stupid.'"
~ Stephanie, 8

"My parents fought all the time. I hid in my room, but I couldn't get away from it. Once, the police came."
~ Sam, 7

"My mom got mad at my dad one day and slammed the door as she left. She never even said goodbye to me and my brothers. Why did she have to do that?"
~ Ryan, 8

"If I come home from something really fun with my dad and I'm in a good mood, my mom gets mad. She thinks I should be mad at him just because she's mad at him."
~ Matt, 14

CHILDREN ON FEELINGS

*"Sometimes I want to run away so
I don't have to face this. They ran
away from it. Why can't I?"*
~ Christy, 9

*"I don't really talk to my parents
about my feelings anymore because
they can't handle it. My mom kept
telling me to not feel sad, but I do
feel sad."*
~ Todd, 12

*"When my dad left, he didn't even
tell us. He was just gone for the
day, then another, and he just never
came back. Finally he called me on
the phone and said he wasn't going
to live with us anymore."*
~ Kevin, 10

CHILDREN CONFUSED BY DIVORCE

"I'm kind of embarrassed about my parents' divorce. I don't know how to tell people."
~ Cara, 11

"It feels like I'm not part of a family anymore."
~Maria, 8

CHILDREN FEELING CAUGHT IN THE MIDDLE

"The other day, my dad said, 'Your mother is taking me to the cleaners.' I felt bad."
~ Kao, 13

"My mom said she wouldn't come to my recital if my dad is there. What am I supposed to do? I finally told him my recital was cancelled, but I don't think he believed me."
~ Jenna, 11

"I cried and told my parents, 'I'll never make you mad again, I promise!' but they said it wasn't me. I know they fought over some of the things I did."
~ *Meghan, 13*

"My dad asked if my mom has a boyfriend. I felt like a trapped animal. I just stood there staring at him. It was awful."
~ *Danny, 13*

"I wanted to go to the basketball game with my dad, but my mom made me feel bad about it."
~ *Raymond, 11*

CHILDREN UNPREPARED

"My mom didn't work before, but now she works full-time. Being alone in the apartment after school is kind of scary."
~ *Dina, 12*

"It makes me feel funny to do things with my dad and his new girlfriend."
~ *Shane, 12*

CHILDREN FEELING REASSURED

*"I thought the divorce was my fault
until my dad told me the reason why.
My parents just don't love each other anymore."*
~ Lisa, 9

*"I wish my parents weren't divorced,
but I know they both love me."*
~ Sean, 12

~EXERCISE~

Your Children

Which statement sounded like something your children might have experienced or said during your divorce or break-up?

_____
_____
_____
_____

What would you like to talk to your children about now that you've heard what other children have to say about divorce?

_____
_____
_____
_____

It's never too late to help your children deal with the emotions of divorce. This 8-week course will equip you with the understanding and tools to do that.

REVIEW OF WEEK 1

- Remember it takes time to create change. Commit the 8 weeks needed to learn collaborative co-parenting.
- Remember that it takes change to make change. Focus on changing yourself rather than trying to change your co-parent. As you implement positive changes, your co-parent may become more willing to change as well.
- To transition from being intimate partners to parenting partners, you must stop blaming, stop indulging in negative thinking, and stop dwelling on the past.
- Letting go of the past means learning to live in the present and look forward, not backward.
- Letting go of the past also leaves you more open to setting goals, taking on new challenges, and facing the future.
- Forgiveness is something you do for yourself and your children. It will lighten the emotional burden you are carrying and make it easier to be a good parent and an effective co-parent.
- Allowing your children to express their feelings sends a message of caring. It also builds trust so they can share other matters with you too.
- Your child's questions give you important information during the divorce process.
- It is important to be a role model who demonstrates how to deal with stress and anger in appropriate ways.
- If your children are having a hard time but don't feel comfortable talking to you about the divorce, arrange for them If

your children are having a hard time but don't feel comfortable talking to you about the divorce, arrange for them to talk to a neutral person, such as a therapist, child specialist, or pastoral counselor.

WEEK 1 ACTION ITEMS

- Complete the exercises in Week 1.
- Repeat the "Letting Go" Affirmations in this chapter several times this week.
- Journal about an event where you had a chance to use the "Tips on How to Respond to your Children's Feelings" or about a challenging event where you wish you had used the tips.

WEEK 2, BUILDING THE COLLABORA-TIVE CO-PARENTING RELATIONSHIP

"The only thing that will redeem mankind is cooperation."
~ Bertrand Russell, philosopher

What You Will Find in Week 2:

- Transitioning from Marriage Partners to Parenting Partners
- Talking to Children About Divorce
- Building Trust Between Co-Parents
- Children's Need for Trust
- Writing a Mission Statement
- Co-Parenting Guidelines
- Collaborative Co-Parenting Meetings
- Guidelines for Holding Meetings

TRANSITIONING FROM MARRIAGE PARTNERS TO PARENTING PARTNERS

The term "co-parenting" is used to describe the relationship between two people who, by mutual agreement or court order after a divorce or breakup, share responsibility for their children's well-being. Add the word "collaborative" to it and it means the two of you are co-parenting with mutual respect, which is the ideal situation for you and, most importantly, your children.

Some people find that collaborative co-parenting is easy while many others struggle to get along—or maybe no one ever told them that parents who were once married *can* get along after divorce. One positive way to look at it is to see the relationship as transitioning from married, intimate partners to "parenting partners."

Making the change from marriage partners to parenting partners requires focusing on the present and letting go of the past. Start by letting go of old resentments, regrets, and blame. Resist the urge to fall back on old patterns of arguing and trying to hurt each other.

Regrets and anger about the past interfere with your ability to parent positively in the present. Having a successful parent partnership requires cooperation. The goal is to manage your children's lives together with a focus on them, rather than on your crises and conflicts.

One couple I worked with came to understand this in a mediation session. I listened as the woman told her estranged husband that she wanted them to get along better because, although they were divorcing, they'd "forever be parenting partners." Her statement seemed to switch on a light in his head and he became much more cooperative after that.

Sometimes just a small adjustment in how you view a situation can change your feelings about it. What these co-parents came to understand about one another is absolutely right: You and your co-parent are going to be parents together for the rest of your lives.

Keep in mind that a healthy parenting partnership puts your children's best interests first. This is the foundation for your children to be nourished and supported by *both* parents.

What is a parenting partnership? It is a business-like relationship between two parents who are able to conduct themselves professionally, collaboratively, and creatively for the sake of their children.

A valuable start is both parents agreeing to form a partnership to work together to provide for the emotional and physical needs of their children.

Forming a Successful Parenting Partnership

- *Once two parents have agreed to form a partnership, the partnership needs some guidelines to work within.*
- *One way to do this is to write a mission statement that captures what your parent partnership is about.*
- *The mission statement helps parents focus on why the partnership is important.*
- *Staying focused on your children also allows you to avoid triggering some of the old emotions and conflict from the marriage relationship.*
- *Having some rules, or guidelines, about how you operate can help your partnership avoid some of the old triggers that plagued your relationship.*

Talking to Children about Divorce

Talking to your children *together* about the

divorce can promote a positive co-parenting relationship. This allows both parents to answer questions and also helps parents avoid blaming each other for the divorce.

Children's reactions are tied to how parents discuss issues related to the divorce or breakup. For this reason, I urge you to think carefully about the words you use.

The following tips can help you handle not only the first discussion with your children about the breakup, but later talks as well:

• Talking to your children about the divorce together will give them a sense they are not going to lose one of their parents.
• Do not keep the divorce a secret or wait until the last minute. You do not want your children to find out about the divorce or other significant changes to their lives from another source besides you.
• Keep things simple and straightforward. Children do not have to be burdened with the details of the divorce process.
• Although divorce is a difficult time, it is important for you to be calm and reassuring when discussing the divorce with your children.
• Children often feel they may be the cause of the divorce. Let them know the divorce is not their fault. This is a message they will need to hear repeatedly from you.
• Tell your children that you both love them and the divorce will not change your love for them.
• Acknowledge that divorce is sad and upsetting for everyone. It's OK to allow time for the sadness, loss, and changes that take place.
• Validate their feelings without trying to fix them or talk your children out of their feelings.
• When talking about the divorce, do not discuss the other parent's faults or problems with your children.

- Avoid arguing or discussing financial issues in front of your children.
- Give children opportunities to have a loving, satisfying relationship with both parents.

Building Trust Between Co-Parents

Trust is important in any relationship, so it makes sense that you and your co-parent must find a way to rebuild trust in this new partnership. If one parent feels that the other is withholding or distorting information, this breaks down trust in the co-parenting relationship. One way to build trust is to keep the agreements and promises you make to the other person.

Imagine business partners failing to share important information about the ups and downs of their business or failing to do what they say they will do in the company. This would be devastating to the company's success. It can hurt your parenting partnership just as much. Trust is key to building a successful partnership.

But what about my co-parent, you ask, and all the things he or she has done—or did in the past? You cannot control how another person behaves, but you can control your own behavior. One person can provide the foundation for a business-like relationship. One person's trustworthiness can make the difference in building a co-parent partnership. Even in business dealings, we may come across people who prove themselves untrustworthy, but that doesn't justify becoming untrustworthy ourselves.

It takes time to rebuild trust—be patient. When my daughter, Jessica, was young, she went to visit her father at his home in busy San Francisco. Her dad took her to a parade and, excited by all the festivities, Jessica wandered away into the crowd.

Her father was frantic, looking everywhere for his little girl. Luckily, Jessica was safe and sound, comforted by a couple that discovered her and kept her calm until she could be reunited with her dad.

When her father returned Jessica to me, he didn't tell me what had happened. In fact, I didn't know a thing until a couple weeks later when Jessica mentioned the nice couple that found her at the parade. She was only four years old at the time.

I was terrified and angry at being in the dark about what had happened, but once I talked to Jessica's dad about it, I could tell he was just as upset as I was, so I pushed myself to trust that he had done his best in the midst of a frightening situation. He agreed to keep me better informed in the future.

I did keep a closer watch on Jessica, checking in frequently when she was away. To his credit, Jessica's dad understood my concern and allowed me to do this because it was clear that we both had Jessica's best interests at heart. We also understood the importance of building a trusting relationship.

Children's Need for Trust

When children know that they can count on and trust the people in their lives, they feel secure and self-confident. Parents earn the trust of their children when their words match their actions. If you make a promise, do all you can to follow through on keeping that promise.

Some of the changes children often witness during divorce are unsettling new emotions and behaviors from their parents. Children who cannot trust their parents to behave like responsible adults have trouble trusting that everything after the divorce will eventually be OK. This is confusing and upsetting to children. One way to minimize upsetting your children is to practice solid co-parenting skills that shield children from the more negative aspects of divorce. A good starting point is to begin your partnership by writing a mission statement.

What Is a Mission Statement?

A written mission statement is something that keeps you focused on the purpose of your partnership. Writing that statement helps you recall what is genuinely important to you — in this case, parenting your children together in the best way possible because your children need both of you.

In my practice, I've found that some parents want to write individual mission statements while others will write their mission statements together. Sometimes one parent writes the mission statement and the other parent adopts it. There is no right way or wrong way. Do what works for you, but as Nike says, "Just do it."

Here are two examples of possible mission statements:

Mission Statement Sample #1

We will work together to provide love, structure, and guidance for our children, Madison and Trevor, with decisions focused on our children's best interests.

Mission Statement Sample #2

Although divorced, I am dedicated to creating a cooperative, interactive, and caring relationship for the benefit of our child. I want to give our child a meaningful relationship with both of us. I affirm that I will always do what's best for our child.

~EXERCISE~

Writing a Mission Statement

Creating a mission statement should include the use of action words (verbs), the standards you want to bring to the mission, and the mission's purpose (who will benefit).

The following is a list of sample action words for your mission statement. You can use some of these or add your own.

Action Words   **Standards**

Purpose:

Who Benefits

Sample Action Words

Communicate, Collaborate, Work Together, Create, Give, Provide, Strengthen, Encourage, Resolve, Cooperate, Work, Educate, Care For, Nurture

---

The standards you incorporate into the mission statement are the values you want to bring to the co-parenting relationship. These include ideas such as dedication, honesty, and understanding. Here are some sample ideas for the standards you adopt:

Sample "Standards" or Values to Incorporate

Love, Caring, Structure, Cooperation, Openness, Integrity, Honesty, Trust, Understanding, Vision, Success, Security, Guidance, Harmony, Self-Worth, Maturity

The purpose of the mission statement, or who benefits, is easy. This is where you insert the names of your children.

Working through the above ideas should provide you with a strong outline for writing your mission statement. Filling in the blanks will show you what you have so far:

1. (Action words) _____
2. (Standards) _____
3. (Purpose) Insert your children's names_____

Use the space below to write your own mission statement. If you like, you can use this formula to help you through the process:

My mission is to:

_____, _____, _____ **(three action words)**

_____ **(your standards or values)**

for my children: _____ **(children's names)**

Now refine your statement in the space below. Glance back at the sample mission statements if you need help.

_____
_____
_____
_____
_____

> *"The most important single ingredient in the formula of success is knowing how to get along with people."*
> *~ Theodore Roosevelt, 26th President of the United States*

Building Confidence in the Co-Parenting Partnership

Once your mission statement is written, focus on the big picture, not minor disagreements or inconveniences. Just remember that although disagreements occur in every partnership, how you handle these differences is what determines success.

Many of my clients are visibly relieved when I advise them to view their relationship with their co-parent as a business relationship instead of a friendship. Viewing your co-parenting partnership as a business relationship is the ideal model for working together to make choices in the best interests of your children after a divorce or breakup.

Perhaps it will help you to think of it this way: You wouldn't let differences with a business partner keep you from reaching a shared goal. When it comes to your family, keep your children and their needs as your focus. Seeing you work through your disagreements will benefit your children as much as it benefits you.

Successful businesses also engage in teambuilding. My business coach, Marlys Thompson, promotes what are called the

Business Coach Marlys Thompson Uses "Six C's for an Effective Team"

Commitment
Consensus
Caring (sincerity)
Communication
Clarity of Roles
Clarity of Goals

"Six C's for an Effective Team." The "Six C's" are commitment, consensus, caring (in the form of being sincere), communication, clarity of roles, and clarity of goals. Stop for a moment and imagine focusing on each of the six ideas in your co-parenting partnership and how that would benefit your children.

Another thing to realize is that business partnerships are often built by bringing different talents together. What this teaches us is that differences have value. Look at any business requiring innovation and you will see that the creative contributions usually come from a diversity of unique personality types.

You can't expect business partners to avoid all conflict or not come to the table with different ideas. In business, partners expect to work through conflict with the understanding that there is always more than one way to do things. That's how things get done—through cooperation and mutual respect. Cooperation and mutual respect are key in every co-parenting relationship too.

> *"We would accomplish many more things if we did not think of them as impossible."*
> ~ *C. Malesherbez, author*

Collaborative Co-Parenting Guidelines

To help your new co-parenting relationship succeed, it's helpful to have some basic guidelines you both agree on in advance. Setting these up before sticky situations arise is easier than trying to resolve challenges or conflict without any guidelines in place.

You likely know your co-parent's hot buttons and he or she probably knows yours, so try to agree on some guidelines in advance that address these problem areas. For instance, if your ex is obsessively early and you're always running behind, set a guideline about calling each other if you're ever going to be more than fifteen minutes late.

Here are some examples of guidelines you might use, but I encourage you to create a personalized list that will work for you.

Collaborative Co-Parenting Guidelines: Examples

- *We will not argue in front of our children.*
- *Children will not be used to transmit messages or money.*
- *We will not say degrading things about the other parent to our children or in front of our children. Children need to respect both parents.*
- *We will ask our families and friends to avoid saying degrading things about either parent to our children.*
- *We will limit our children's contact with "toxic" friends or relatives who are not willing to be supportive or who criticize either parent in front of our children.*
- *If a parent picking up or dropping off a child is going to be more than fifteen minutes late, he or she will call to notify the other parent.*
- *We will both try to accommodate schedule changes needed by the other parent as much as is reasonably possible.*
- *We will accommodate our children's activities whenever possible so they don't have to change their lives because of divorce.*
- *We will work together to create guidelines for raising our child.*
- *All items taken from one parent's home to the other's household will travel back and forth with the child, especially important items such as sports uniforms, glasses, favorite blankets, coats, school books, musical instruments, and favorite toys.*
- *We will check with each other when our child expresses a complaint about one of us in order to hear the adult version.*
- *We will respect each other's privacy and not use our children as informers or spies.*
- *We will divide ongoing responsibilities. For instance, maybe Dad takes the children for all their haircuts and back-to-school shopping while Mom takes the children to all routine medical and dental checkups.*
- *We will not discuss emotional issues regarding the breakup or anger at each other with the children.*

Weekly Updates

Weekly updates are important in keeping both co-parents informed about the needs of the children. Make it a point to exchange a call or e-mail each week—generally at the same day or time. Keep it brief. Stick with the business at hand and discuss child-related issues. Always include something positive about the children, as well as the challenges. End with a statement of gratitude or thanks for the ability to have open dialogue.

In running my business, I meet every week with my office manager and these meetings are priceless for keeping me updated about what's going on and important decisions I need to make to keep the business thriving and growing. The length of the meeting is determined by how much information there is to share. The exchange of information is vital to the success of my business.

This business-meeting concept works well with co-parenting. When my daughter Jessica was growing up, I talked to her father by telephone on a regular basis to keep him informed of her progress. He did the same for me.

Keeping him posted on what our daughter was doing at school, in sports, and in her extracurricular activities gave the two of them wonderful conversation topics that helped them build a strong relationship.

Tips for Weekly Updates

- *Make it a point to exchange a call or e-mail each week—generally the same day or time.*
- *Keep it brief. Stick with the business at hand—only discuss child-related issues.*
- *Include something positive about the child, as well as the challenges.*
- *End with a statement of gratitude, or thanks, for the ability to have open dialogue.*

These conversations helped me too. During a regular co-parenting phone update, for instance, Jessica's father shared that Jessica had mentioned that her soccer shoes were too tight. I checked and, sure enough, they were too small. For some reason, Jessica had forgotten to tell me, but through her father's open communication with me, the problem was resolved.

Collaborative Co-Parenting Meetings

It's important to hold co-parenting meetings to make sure you're both on the same page about important issues involving your children. The frequency, location, and time of the meeting should be based on what parents agree to and what needs to be discussed. Choose a neutral location. Allow enough time for both parents to express their concerns.

Parents often say that children are their most important treasure. Setting aside an hour or so as needed to deal with the most important part of our life is a valuable investment of time.

The details of these meetings vary, depending on your situation. Parents often look at how well their children are doing to determine if a meeting needs to take place, or how long it might be. Sometimes just an update call or e-mail to confirm that things are going well is all you need. In fact, some parents prefer to handle most communication by e-mail because it allows them to think through everything they want to say — and say what they really mean rather than react to possible hot-button topics.

Requesting a Co-Parenting Meeting

When you need to meet to discuss an issue of concern, try to calm your emotions before placing the call to your co-parent. Then begin by saying something like: "When would be a good time to talk about _____?"

Identify the topic of concern so the other parent is not left wondering about the reason for the meeting. Allow the other parent to identify a time that will work for him or her. If your co-parent refuses to schedule a meeting, explain that the issue is important for the children's sake and needs to be addressed by the two of you as co-parents.

The more conflict there is between you, the more structure you'll likely need. As co-parents you should assess and determine the amount of structure you need to have a successful meeting.

It's important to remember that holding regular meetings to discuss business is what successful business partners do. In this case, your "business" is your children's well-being.

Even Horses Benefit from Cooperation

Let me tell you a story about a teacher trying to teach co-operation to his students. One day in class, the teacher threw out the fact that a draft horse can pull one to three tons of weight. "Given that," he said, "what would you expect *two* draft horses to be able to pull?"

The students talked among themselves, and using simple mathematics, they came with the answer of two to six tons. Double the horses, double the power. Simple, right?

"No," the teacher answered. "A single draft horse can pull one to three tons, but two draft horses, in tandem, can pull twelve to fourteen tons."

Through cooperation, you always will be able to achieve more and achieve it more quickly, so create a team and pull together.

When Issues Won't Wait

About the only things that can't be handled in meetings are emergencies. These could be actual emergencies such as a child's medical injury or simply unforeseen issues that need to be addressed before the next meeting. Such circumstances often require a phone call. So that's what you do: call.

Emergency Calls

What constitutes an emergency? Having a solid understanding between co-parents about what constitutes an emergency is a good idea. In general, the following may be a guideline until you have a consensus with your co-parent about what an emergency is:

- Illness (reason enough to keep your child out of school)
- Injury
- Serious problems at school or elsewhere
- Any situation that would put your child at risk
- Any other agreed-upon emergency

Placing an Emergency Call

1. Stay calm. Do not be an alarmist.

2. Be specific. Just tell your co-parent what happened.

3. Discuss with your co-parent what needs to happen next.

4. Express what help you need from your co-parent.

5. Decide together what each parent's follow-through will be.

6. Stay Calm. Do not be an alarmist. This when your child needs to sense your calmness.

7. Be specific. Just tell your co-parent what happened.

8. Explain to your co-parent what needs to happen next.

9. Express what help you need from your co-parent.

10. Decide together what the agreed follow-up or follow-through is.

Annual Meetings

The annual meeting between the two of you is best held in person. It's very helpful to have a written agenda, even if it's just a few notes jotted down. Stick with the agenda or child-related issues. Do not discuss any other issues at this time, including financial issues, unless they are child-related. It may be helpful to place a photo of your children on the table during the meeting.

Annual meetings are important because they give you a chance to discuss your children's developmental stages and needs, which change from year to year.

Setting an Agenda

Setting an agenda for your co-parent meetings allows you to talk about one issue at a time rather than having fragmented conversations.

Setting an agenda is fairly easy. Before the meeting, each of you should make a list of the following:

- New issues
- Issues left over from the last meeting
- Goals you want to achieve at this meeting

Both of you should contribute to the agenda. One of you can combine the issues prior to the meeting, or you can each bring a list. If you both are very comfortable with using e-mail, that's often the easiest way to share and combine items for the agenda. List the easy issues first and the most difficult issues last.

Holding the Meeting

The following guidelines are adapted from the Sacramento Collaborative Practice Group's "Ground Rules for the Collaborative Process" and outline how to behave in a collaborative meeting. I like them because they are just as useful as guidelines for co-parenting meetings.

Keeping on track will be less of an issue if you follow your agenda. Instead of trying to discuss all of the things on the agenda at once, discuss one at a time and work your way down the list. If one item becomes difficult, come back to it if you both agree on that. Pace yourself so you don't run out of time and not get to the most difficult issues.

If a past issue has been resolved, be sure to mention it and congratulate yourselves.

At the meeting, make sure you are both on the same wavelength by listening to the other parent and only having one person speak at a time.

Doing This for Your Children

When getting along seems difficult, keep in mind that you are doing all of this for your children. All children deserve to feel secure. Making your co-parenting partnership work well helps children see that they still have two parents and a family.

~ EXERCISE ~

Your Co-Parent Relationship

1. Take a moment to write about a time you co-parented well.

_____

_____

_____

_____

2. What can you do to improve the trust in your co-parent relationship?

_____

_____

_____

_____

3. What are some other ways you can improve your co-parent relationship?

_____

_____

_____

_____

REVIEW OF WEEK 2

- Creating a successful co-parenting partnership requires transitioning from old relationship resentments, regrets, and blame — and putting your children's interests first.
- If you haven't yet told your children about the divorce, talk to them together and avoid blaming each other.
- A mission statement keeps you focused on the purpose of your partnership and helps you recall what is genuinely important.
- A mission statement should include action words (such as *communicate* and *educate*), standards and values (such as *trust* and *understanding*), and the reason for writing the statement (your children).
- A collaborative parenting partnership is more like a business relationship than a friendship.
- To help your co-parent develop trust in your new partnership, keep your promises and avoid withholding important information.

- When children know that they can count on the people in their lives, they feel secure and self-confident. Parents earn children's trust by keeping promises.
- It is important to establish co-parenting guidelines, such as:
  - We will not argue in front of our children.
  - We will respect each other's privacy.
  - We will divide ongoing responsibilities.
- Weekly co-parenting updates should be brief and should focus on child-related issues.
- When requesting a business meeting, you should identify the topic of concern, agree on a convenient time, and choose a neutral location.
- An emergency call is needed when your child is sick enough to miss school or a situation has arisen that could put your child at risk.
- When you place the emergency call, you should stay calm, be specific, and decide together what should be done.
- It's best if the annual meeting is held in person and based on an agenda.
- An agenda will help you discuss one issue at a time and stay on track.

WEEK 2 ACTION ITEMS

- Complete the exercises in Week 2.
- Memorize your "Mission Statement" and repeat it silently to yourself several times this week.
- Journal about an event where you had a chance to use the "Collaborative Co-Parenting Guidelines: Examples" in this chapter or about a challenging event where you wish you had used the guidelines.

WEEK 3, RESOLVING CONFLICT

"Whenever you're in conflict with someone, there is one factor that can make the difference between damaging your relationship and deepening it. That factor is attitude."
~ William James, American philosopher

What You Will Find in Week 3:

• Conflict in Divorce and Breakups
• How Divorce Affects Children
• Tools for Communication
• Positive Body Language
• Choosing the Right Words
• How to Keep People From Pushing Your Buttons
• Choosing Your Battles
• Flexibility
• Value the Ongoing Relationship

CONFLICT IN DIVORCE AND BREAKUPS

When we're in conflict with the people closest to us, our defensive responses are often intensified. It is the people we know best, such as our spouses, children, and parents, who arouse our deepest emotions. Society leads us to believe that it's best to avoid conflict. This often leaves us with very few skills to resolve problems when they do arise. Sometimes it is not the conflict that causes the problem, but the way we respond to the conflict.

Take a look at how one couple addresses a problem and the larger conflict it creates:

- Sheena is upset because Mike refuses to discuss who should pay for back-to-school clothes for the children, something they didn't cover in their parenting plan.
- Mike withdraws and ignores Sheena's requests to talk. Mike believes that talking about this will lead to a fight.
- Sheena resents that Mike is controlling the situation by refusing to listen to her, so she pushes harder to get Mike to listen. Her voice-mail messages become louder and more demanding.
- When Mike doesn't listen now, she escalates the situation, perhaps getting her attorney involved or saying bad things about him to the children.
- Mike feels attacked. He retaliates by saying bad things about Sheena in front of the children.
- Open war results.

What if Mike had listened to Sheena's feelings and concerns? What if Sheena understood Mike's withdrawing as a way to avoid a fight? What if this couple had better ways to communicate and listen to one another about problems?

How Divorce Affects Children

Learning to resolve conflicts with your co-parent is important for the well-being of your children. Children exposed to destructive parental conflict show signs of increased stress and confusion, which affects their ability to function at their best.

"The goal is to shelter your children from any conflict that arises between you, their parents."
~ Carol Delzer, course author

This stress can affect their self-esteem, schoolwork, and relationships with their peers. Research has shown that children who experience conflict between their parents are more likely to have conflicts with others, such as teachers, friends, parents, and siblings.

Divorce can be a difficult time for children. Many children go through the divorce process with a minimal amount of harm and make reasonable adjustments to the changes in their lives. Children who are significantly affected by divorce and have a difficult time coping have problems primarily from exposure to parental conflict. Your goal should be to shelter your children from any conflict that arises between you, their parents.

Age is another significant factor in how a child reacts to the changes that come with divorce:

- Infants and toddlers do not have the ability to understand what divorce is. If parents are able to adjust within a reasonable time, the infant or toddler will feel few, if any, effects of the divorce.
- In children ages three to five years old, parents should watch for a loss of normal cheerfulness or curiosity. Parents should insulate children from marital conflict and divorce issues and be careful about how they discuss the divorce process with children of this age.

- Children ages six to twelve can display increased anxiety, restlessness, over-activity, moodiness, tantrums, or aggression. Again, parents should insulate the children from marital conflict and divorce issues and be careful about how they discuss the divorce process with children of this age.

- For teenagers ages thirteen to eighteen, parents need to watch for withdrawal from the family, social isolation, involvement with anti-social activities with peers, low self-esteem, and intense feelings of loss or helplessness. Parental cooperation in dealing with teenagers' problems at the time of divorce is crucial. Like younger children, teenagers need the support of both parents. Parents also need to avoid using teens as confidants during or after the divorce — even if teens encourage it. Sometimes teenagers align with one parent during or after a divorce. Parents should be careful not to allow teens to take sides. It is in their best interest to maintain close ties to both parents.

With children of all ages, your job is to minimize negative impacts. In some cases, children may require professional counseling to adjust to the changes they are experiencing.

Understanding the Creative Value in Conflict

Yes, there really is value in conflict. That may sound contradictory, but conflict is a natural and valuable part of life. It teaches us to consider different points of view when making decisions. Your children also learn from watching how you and your co-parent work through problems together. Turning destructive conflict into constructive solutions allows you to make the most effective decisions about your children's lives.

But how do you do that?

Conflict resolution begins with a central goal: to find solutions through constructive exchange. The key is to move conflict away from a destructive process toward a constructive one. Take the example of a mom who is angry that the favorite videos she sends with their toddler to Dad's house always get left behind. She accuses her co-parent of keeping the videos so he doesn't have to spend money on videos himself. This is a destructive way to communicate what she really wants. A more constructive way to address this problem would be for her to say what she expects without pointing fingers: "I'd really appreciate it if you'd remember to pack the videos in Tyler's backpack when he leaves your house. I will do the same so we don't have to buy two sets."

> ## Resolving Conflict
>
> *Resolving conflict requires you to:*
> * *Communicate effectively*
> * *Act in good faith*
> * *Be open-minded*
> * *Negotiate in a safe environment*

Be willing to engage in conflict as long as the conversation remains respectful and focuses on solutions. If you are truly willing to hear different points of view and are open to all creative input, you can produce positive change and growth. One of the keys to doing this successfully is improving your communication skills.

Tools for Communication

TOOL 1: LISTEN

We all want to be heard, but being heard works both ways. Too many of us only half listen to others while our eyes glaze over and we prepare what we plan to say next. In response, people recognize that they're not really being heard and they turn us off.

By not fully listening to others, we miss opportunities to learn and grow. It's hard to be successful with only a portion of the information you need about a situation. We've all slipped into moments of tuning out other people, especially when what they're saying is something we're reluctant to hear. Have you ever:

- Listened just long enough until the other person "slips up" so you can gather ammunition for an attack? That's the "I've gotcha" method of listening.
- Listened just long enough so the other person will be obligated to listen to you?
- Listened just long enough to buy time while you plan what you're going to next?

If you answered "Yes" to any of the above questions, in those situations you're not really listening at all. Good listening also means giving feedback, such as "Is this what you mean?" or "Are you saying...?" The good news is, when people feel listened to, they respond in kind. Most importantly, you may actually learn something that will help you or your children.

This happened to Art and me at a drop-off meeting once when Jessica was twelve years old. I took a deep breath to slow down and show him, with eye contact and positive body language, that the issue I wanted to discuss was important to me—to us, actually.

"Would it work for you, now that Jessica's twelve, for her to be home alone after school from about 3:30 to 5:30 when I get home from work?" Art responded that this didn't feel right to him. I might have gotten upset with him and started to complain about his indifference

Listening Skills

- *Look directly into the other person's eyes.*
- *Lean forward.*
- *Reflect back what you hear the person say.*
- *Ask questions if you're not sure what they mean.*
- *Do not get caught up in being right or making the other person wrong.*

to my schedule and Jessica's push for a little more independence. Instead, I repeated what I heard him say: "I hear that it doesn't feel right to you that Jessica will be home alone for a couple of hours after school at her age. Tell me more about what you are thinking."

She is an only child home alone, for starters, he explained, and he doubted she had the discipline to stay on task and get her homework done. There had to be a better solution.

I said that I agreed with him, but didn't know what the solution was. "What about the neighbor kid, Emily?" he asked. "Hasn't her mother been asking Jessica to baby-sit? Maybe she can go there and baby-sit, which would keep her busy with a responsibility while helping our situation so she's not home alone."

It was a great idea and that's exactly what we did. But I had to be open to it. Coming to agreement required that I listen with an open mind to Art's ideas rather than get caught up in my idea about being right.

I also saw that when we delivered this idea as a team to Jessica, it was accepted more willingly. In fact, now that I look back on it, it was she who had been pushing so hard to be allowed to stay home alone and, while I hadn't been strong enough to say "no" outright, together Art and I were a force she listened to. This is the power of co-parenting, especially when it comes to teens and pre-teens.

TOOL 2: CREATE CLEAR, EFFECTIVE MESSAGES

A wrong word at the wrong time during a conflict is like gasoline on a fire. To communicate with your co-parent effectively, it's important to send clear messages.

One of the best tools for effective, non-combative communication is using "I statements" instead of "You statements." "I statements" are a way of communicating a problem to another person without accusing them of causing the problem.

The formula for "I statements" works like this:
Formula: I feel + (emotion) + (when)
Example: I feel worried when you and Sarah are late.
Some "I statements" also include the effect the situation has on the speaker.
Formula: I feel + (emotion) + (when) + (why)
Example: I feel worried when you and Sarah are late because I think there might have been an accident.

Speaking from your own perspective helps eliminate defensive responses from your co-parent. It also gives the other person room to own up to his or her role in the problem.

Using Observations, Thoughts, Feelings, and Requests to Express Yourself

Another tool I'd like you to try is expressing yourself using observations, thoughts, feelings, and requests. The following box shows this idea in action.

Instead of saying:	**A better way of communicating this idea :**
"You've got to stop letting the kids stay up after 9 o'clock on school nights. It's like you don't care about them doing well in school."	• *"I noticed the kids seem to be tired in school lately." (Observation)* • *"I was thinking it might be best for the children if both of us stuck to a 9 o'clock bedtime on school nights." (Thoughts)* • *"I feel worried that the children might not do well in school if they stay up past 9 o'clock on school nights." (Feelings)* • *"I would appreciate it if we could both stick to a 9 o'clock bedtime on school nights so the children aren't tired in school the next day." (Request)*

TOOL 3: STAND UP FOR YOURSELF

Sometimes we fail to stand up for ourselves and it leaves us feeling frustrated. Other times, we overreact and cause people to withdraw from us. In both instances, we don't get what we need.

The good news is you don't have to either overreact or ignore your feelings. Learning to use assertive communication skills will allow you to be respectful of other points of view while honoring yourself. Assertive communication involves these three elements:

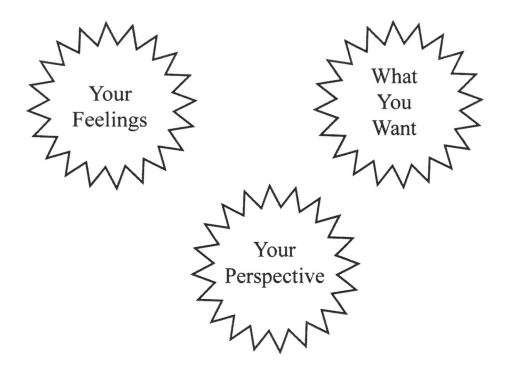

Expressing your feelings means telling your co-parent how you feel about something. Example: I feel embarrassed when your half of the child care payment is paid late to the daycare center.

Expressing what you want means being specific. Example: I would appreciate it if you would pay our daycare center on time.

Expressing your perspective means describing your stance on the issue as your unique point of view. Example: I'm worried that the daycare center will ask us to leave if we don't pay on time.

TOOL 4: KEEP YOUR BODY LANGUAGE OPEN

Your body language communicates a great deal. Hostile postures and facial expressions invite a similar response. To reassure your co-parent of your willingness to cooperate, keep your body language open.

How do you do this? First, make good eye contact so the other person knows you are listening. In reality, this will also help you to become a better listener. Don't fold your arms or turn away, signaling you have shut the other person off.

Work on leaning in toward other people, looking directly in their eyes. Allow them to speak uninterrupted while you nod positively. They will feel truly heard and respected and be more open to what you have to say. Try this with your co-parent. You will be surprised at how far these techniques go toward improving communications and resolving the conflict between you.

TOOL 5: CHOOSING YOUR WORDS AND TONE

Words can heal and words can hurt. The tone of your voice can impact the meaning of words. Those engaged in destructive conflict often choose fighting words and a tone of conflict. In contrast, those engaged in constructive conflict choose their words and tone wisely. How do you do this?

First, slow down your emotions and think about what you are truly thinking, feeling, wanting, and needing at that moment. Sometimes it helps to slow down so much you begin with something like "Thank you for meeting with me" or "I appreciate your willingness to talk about this subject." Speaking with a compassionate tone will help the other person listen more carefully and openly. Choosing a tone that is non-threatening and kind will bring about positive results.

By keeping your words positive rather than using angry words, you will keep the door to dialogue open and allow positive negotiation to take place.

How to Keep People from Pushing Your Buttons

Do some people seem really good at pushing your buttons? In the midst of divorce, the person most likely to do this is your ex-spouse, even if that person doesn't mean to. It's important that you learn to manage negative knee-jerk reactions. When someone says or does something that sets you on the defense, rather than fight, flee, or freeze, learn to respond differently. To do this, you must understand how your buttons are pushed in the first place.

We are responsible for our responses. We choose how to react. How, then, do we keep people from pushing our buttons? First, ask for a break in order to cool down. During that time, reflect on what's really important to you and in the best interests of your children. Then try to see the other person as someone with a valuable point of view rather than someone whose opinion you have to conquer. Finally,

> ### How Fear and Ego Push Our Buttons
>
> 1. *A situation pushes your buttons.*
>   *Example: Your co-parent is late.*
> 2. *You have a belief about the situation.*
>   *"I feel my co-parent is disrespectful of my time."*
> 3. *Your response is negative.*
>   *Example: You find yourself angry, judgmental, and ready to start an argument—prior to knowing why your co-parent is late.*

be committed to the present relationship even though the marital relationship is over. Remember, you are raising children together. That's your most important priority.

The bottom line is that people don't really push our buttons. We push our own buttons by the choices we make. You can choose not to let your buttons be pushed.

Choose Your Battles Carefully

Sometimes we argue over issues of little significance. Before you engage in conflict, ask yourself, is this battle really worth my time and energy? Is this conflict about my children's well-being or safety, or is it more about me feeling wronged and needing to be right?

It's always best to let go of issues unless there is real harm. Arguing over every little issue only diminishes your credibility when a more serious topic needs addressing. Next thing you know, the other person will begin to think you are overly sensitive and will stop taking you seriously.

If you're not sure if the battle is worth engaging, ask yourself how much energy will this conflict take? Always choose to reserve your energy for issues that really matter.

And finally, put your concerns into perspective. Ask yourself if this issue is going to be important in the long run. Will it really matter a year from now? If you can answer yes, then it's probably worth a serious discussion. Now you know how to choose your battles rather than letting them choose you.

Flexibility

If you are determined to stick to your position because you must be right, you are not being flexible. If you're open to the possibility that the other person's ideas may actually work for everyone, you are truly being flexible.

Being flexible requires learning to listen with an open mind. If you refuse to judge or criticize the other person's ideas, you may find new insight into resolving the conflict.

Being flexible also allows you both to find a compromise between two ideas, or perhaps to realize that one idea really is better than the other for your children. It's OK if the idea doesn't happen to be your own. Remember, it's not about winning or losing. It's about creating a winning situation for your children, and flexibility is crucial to the outcome.

Interest-Based Motives vs. Position-Based Motives

When dealing with conflict, distinguish interest-based motives from position-based motives. Understanding where these motives come from will help you resolve conflict.

An ***interest-based motive*** *is flexible, accommodating, and serves the interest at hand.* *The delivery of an interest-based motive is often open, friendly, compassionate, and concerning.*	A ***position-based motive*** *is rigid, sometimes vengeful, and often self-serving.* *The delivery of a position-based motive is often bitter, angry, and offensive to others.*
Example: *Maria usually drives her son, Joe, an hour away to his father's house every other Saturday morning. Maria asks Joe's father, Jose, to change the scheduled drop-off Saturday morning because it will be Joe's first chance to play in his team's soccer match.*	*Example:* *Maria usually drives her son, Joe, an hour away to his father's house every other Saturday morning. Maria tells Joe's father, Jose, that he must attend their son's soccer game because it's required. Secretly, though, she doesn't want to make the one-hour drive.*
This request is about the child, Joe.	*This request is about the mother, Maria.*

When dealing with conflict, ask yourself why this particular issue is important to you. For example, if you are making a request for more parent time with your children, ask yourself why. If the answer is you want increased parenting time because you want more support, then this is a position-based decision. If you think it would be for the children's benefit, this is an interest-based decision.

Knowing the difference between interest-based and position-based decisions will help you think more clearly. Keep the children's best interests in the forefront of your mind. This will help you resolve conflict more meaningfully and fairly.

Good-Faith Negotiations

We all negotiate. We do it every day. Whether it's the price we are willing to pay for a car or deciding how chores will be divided in our household, we negotiate. Some people do not have negotiation skills. Sometimes it's due to a lack of experience, but in many cases it's because they fear conflict.

Winning at all costs is also not a model for good-faith negotiations. The other person, in this case your co-parent, also has ideas worth hearing. Listening to others expands the possibilities for solutions.

If one of you feels you've "lost" while the other has "won," you are not engaging in good-faith negotiations. An old saying holds that if two people walk away from a conflict and one is ecstatic while the other feels defeated,

> **Three Things to Take into Negotiations**
>
> 1. *Understand the benefits and detriments of your ideas.*
> 2. *Be open to other ideas.*
> 3. *Have a Plan B that would work for you.*

it wasn't a fair deal. However, if they both walk away a little unhappy but generally satisfied, it likely was a fair compromise.

How do you negotiate wisely? The key factors are to be open and prepared.

Once you know where you stand, begin to brainstorm ideas together. Be open to all points and ideas during this time. Don't judge. Let the ideas flow. Once you've accomplished that, bring up your desired outcome, using your listening skills to hear your co-parent's thoughts. Propose a compromise and, lastly, resolve the situation.

If you get to this last step and you and your co-parent still disagree, take a break and then go back to the beginning, brainstorming new ideas until a compromise is reached. If this seems hard to do, remember your common interest—what's best for your children.

Creating a Safe Environment for Negotiations

There are three things you can do to create an environment likely to produce good results.

First, **set a time** for your negotiations. "I'd like to talk to you about Sarah's homework schedule. When would be a good time for you?"

Second, **choose a neutral location** so no one feels like they have an advantage, especially if conflict is a problem. You can meet in a park or café. The key is finding a place that both of you feel is a good spot for fair negotiations to take place.

Third, if things get too tense, **take a time out**. Set aside a cool-down moment or even reschedule the talk for another time.

Value the Ongoing Relationship

Another thing to keep in mind in family disputes is to put value on the ongoing relationship even though the relationship is changing through divorce or breakup. Remember that you will spend the rest of your life interacting with your co-parent. There will be celebrations that you both attend to honor your children, such as graduations, weddings, and the births of grandchildren. Imagine what it will be like if all these wonderful life events also make your stomach churn in anger or nervousness years from now because you never resolved the conflict of your breakup. Or imagine the unnecessary turmoil this will cause your children at joyful family events, such as weddings. Do you really want them to have to worry about whether their parents will cause a scene at the reception? If you start to value the co-parent relationship for what it is now, these events will be more pleasant for you and your children in the future.

Who Me?

A valuable approach for understanding what creates conflict between you and your co-parent is looking at what you are doing to contribute to the disagreement, but be careful how you analyze this. If one person throws stones into the water and the other person throws more stones into the water, it can be hard to determine which stones are actually creating the ripples.

One person can change the direction of conflict by changing his or her reaction and contribution to the conflict.

Humor Can Be Hurtful

A sense of humor can help us through difficult times, but it can also hurt another person. One of my most upsetting experiences as a co-parent resulted from a "joke" that my co-parent Art played on me.

Our daughter Jessica regularly spent time with her dad, who owned an apartment building with a self-serve laundry. One weekend when Jessica was with him, Art realized his support payment was due *and* that he had not deposited the quarters from the laundry. He asked Jessica to help him count quarters. They spent the entire Saturday afternoon counting piles of change and by the end of the day had counted out the entire support payment in quarters.

With great laughter (and proud of himself, I'm sure), Art shared with Jessica that this was money for her mother and that Jessica was to be sure to tell her how they had counted it out themselves—and the exact amount of support was in the bag.

When Art and I met at our usual meeting place the next day, he mentioned that he had the support payment with him. He asked me to open the trunk of my car so he could put

Jessica's things inside. Art then asked Jessica to help him lift a large triple-weight paper bag, as I looked on in bewilderment. The bag was so heavy Art could barely lift it. He placed it in the trunk, weighing down the rear end of my car so much it lowered it by several inches.

When I asked what was in the bag, Art said it was my support and that Jessica would verify it was all there. Before I could say a word, he jumped in his car and drove away laughing. I stood there stunned. I looked in the bag and, to my amazement, saw thousands of loose quarters. I was so angry I began to cry and swear. I'm ashamed to admit that I called Art some pretty bad names in front of Jessica that day.

Once we got home, the bag was too heavy for me to carry inside. I went to the bank the next day during my lunch break. I asked for help carrying the bag inside, but the bank clerk said they could not accept loose quarters as a deposit. Bank policy said the coins had to be counted and grouped into rolls to be deposited.

That evening after I put Jessica to bed, I took a large bowl, walked out to the car, and over and over again scooped out bowls of quarters, which I then took inside to roll. It took me four days to get all the quarters rolled. Art was right; the entire support payment was there.

After I cooled down, I wrote Art the following letter:

Dear Art,

I was so angry on Sunday to receive my support in a paper bag full of quarters. Having Jessica spend your parenting time counting support seems like a cruel and unfit use of your precious time with her.

I ask that you never discuss support or the exchange of support in her presence again. This causes confusion and emotional strain for children, which is entirely unnecessary.

From now on, I want you to send the support to my office in a timely manner. If you ever give me quarters again, I will consider it a gift and request that you pay the unpaid support.

If you are feeling resentful about paying support, I will be glad to discuss this with you and provide you with information to justify my needs for support.

Your future cooperation will be greatly appreciated.

Sincerely,

Carol

As you can imagine, Art wasn't going to let me have the last word, so he wrote me the following letter:

Dear Carol,

I would suggest you take the bag of quarters and buy yourself a sense of humor. For God's sake, Carol, what is with you? It was meant as a joke.

I always let Jessica count quarters from the laundry because she likes doing it. While she was counting quarters last week, I asked her whether we should give some to her mommy. She thought it was fun until you ruined it for her. The only thing that was cruel and unfit is you taking the fun out of it. If anything has caused emotional strain and confusion for Jessica, it's your name-calling and bitter attitude.

Have some gratitude that I always pay your support and that I always pay it on time.

Have a nice day, and may God bless you!

Art

As I think back on the quarter episode and re-read the old letters, the entire situation makes me laugh out loud. But I can assure you, I was not laughing at the time. Back then, I was a busy single mother with better things to do than spend four evenings rolling quarters. So while it's important to maintain a sense of humor, be careful how you use it.

~ EXERCISE ~

Conflict Reflection

Ask yourself the questions listed below. Take a moment to think about them and then write down your answers. Regarding the last conflict you had with your co-parent (or the issue you argue over time and time again):

• What did you do to contribute to the conflict?

_____

• What would you do differently in the future?

_____

• What can you do now to reduce the conflict?

_____

• What could you do next time conflict occurs to make it constructive?

_____

REVIEW OF WEEK 3

• The people we know best, including our spouse and children, often arouse our deepest emotions and defenses.
• Learning to resolve conflicts with your co-parent is important for the well-being of your children.

- When children are exposed to destructive parental conflict, they show signs of stress and confusion. Their self-esteem, schoolwork, and relationships can be affected.
- Conflict is a natural and valuable part of life. It teaches us to consider different points of view when making decisions.
- Resolving conflict requires you to act in good faith, communicate effectively, be open-minded, and negotiate in a safe environment.
- To become a better listener, lean forward and make eye contact, repeat or rephrase what you heard the other person say, and ask questions if there's anything you don't understand.
- It's easier to resolve conflicts if you use "I statements" ("I worry when you're late") rather than "You statements" ("You are always late").
- When you communicate assertively, you express your feelings, your perspective, and what you want.
- To make conflict constructive rather than destructive, use a non-threatening tone, choose your words carefully, and be open to your co-parent discussing the issue.
- You can avoid overreacting when your co-parent pushes your buttons by taking a brief break to cool down and reflecting on what's in your children's best interests.
- Before engaging in conflict, ask yourself:
  o Is this battle really significant?
  o Is it about my children's well-being or safety?
  o Will it matter a year from now?
- An interest-based motive is flexible and accommodating, and it serves everyone's interests.
- A position-based motive is rigid, self-serving, and sometimes vengeful.
- To negotiate successfully, you should understand the benefits and detriments of your ideas, be open to other ideas, and have a Plan B that would work for you.

• To create a safe environment for negotiating, set a specific meeting time, choose a neutral location, and take a break to cool down if necessary.

WEEK 3 ACTION ITEMS

• Complete the exercises in Week 3.
• Try using the "Tools for Communication" in this chapter and journal about how these tools worked for you.
• Journal about an event that pushed your buttons and how you responded to it.

WEEK 4, MANAGING EMOTIONS

What You Will Find in Week 4:

- Exploring Emotions
- How to Distinguish Fear from Wisdom
- Tools for Managing Emotions
- The Importance of Movement
- The Importance of a Healthy Diet
- Using Meditation to Manage Emotions
- Understanding Fear
- Understanding Anger
- Operating From a Place of Wisdom
- Setting Goals

"He who is afraid of a thing
gives it power over him."
~ Moorish proverb

EXPLORING EMOTIONS

In the School of Life, a relationship breakup can be one of our greatest challenges and lessons. Ending a relationship is often painful. If you didn't want the relationship to end, moving on can be especially difficult. Such situations can stir up strong feelings of fear and anger. When fear consumes you, it paralyzes your thinking. When you are operating out of fear, it is more difficult to make important choices for you and your children. This week we'll give you tools to help manage your emotions so you can negotiate your breakup more easily and be a better parent.

You may have concerns about your ability to let go of the emotions you are feeling during this intense time. Perhaps in the past you've had difficulty making healthy emotional choices under stress. Your history doesn't matter if you make the commitment to move forward by understanding what triggers your emotions. Let's explore what emotions are, why they sometimes get the best of us, and what to do about it.

It is important to understand that our feelings are normal reactions to the world around us. Having emotions is part of what makes us human. How we *act* on those feelings is what produces good or bad results.

Strong feelings like the ones that often occur in divorce can be overwhelming and unfamiliar. When something feels unfamiliar, we sometimes react with fear or even anger. Those churning emotions can make you feel confused and out of control, doing and saying things that will cause more harm.

One helpful way to gain control over negative emotions is to name the feelings. The part of the brain responsible for emotions is different from the part responsible for language, so naming the feeling can help you gain some distance from it. Once you've identified the emotion you're feeling as anger, fear, sadness, or something else, it's easier to come up with a game plan to deal with it.

We will look into the emotions of fear and anger more closely later in this chapter, but the main thing to understand right now is the importance of separating a feeling from an action. Acting inappropriately as a result of overpowering emotions results in increased conflict. Intense emotions lead us to create stories that are not complete or true. Intense emotions make us believe: "It's all his fault." "She's trying to ruin me." "He has no parenting skills." These are the stories told by intense emotions. The truth is much different, but we cannot see it when we're blinded by overpowering emotions.

Assessing those overblown stories your emotions tell you will keep you from acting on them. Emotions come and go, but actions have consequences. It's better to cool down and act on the basis of what's true rather than just venting your emotions. Venting might make you feel better momentarily, but calming your emotions instead of reacting will be best for you and your children in the long run.

Here are some examples of assessing emotional statements:

Statement	Assessment
"It's all his fault."	*Is it really ALL his fault?*
"She's trying to ruin me."	*Maybe she did something you're angry about, but is she really trying to RUIN you?*
"He has no parenting skills."	*Maybe he does a few things differently from you, but does he really have NO parenting skills?*

The Leaver Versus the Leavee

Another important factor is the emotional difference that often exists between the parent who left the relationship (the leaver) and the parent who was left behind (the leavee). In many cases, the leaver has been considering divorce for a while and may have already worked through the feelings of loss and disappointment. This can make the leaver seem without emotion or even cavalier once the breakup occurs. This can further hurt the leavee if that person's feelings about the breakup are new and raw. What is really going on in such scenarios is the two people are at different emotional stages of the relationship breakup.

I often ask divorcing spouses, "Whose decision was it to end the marriage?" This valuable information often tells me where they are emotionally. When their feelings are far apart, that emotional distance may be at the root of their conflict.

If a spouse did not make the decision to end the relationship, there can be anger, fear, disappointment, and resentment. These emotions will show up as a challenge in working together to develop a parenting plan or reaching agreements about the children. Being aware of these emotions can help you work toward accepting and understanding them. This will help you set them aside so you can work toward a healthy co-parenting relationship. Your children will benefit and so will you and your co-parent.

Making Choices from Wisdom Instead of Fear

Studies show that divorce, the death of a loved one, moving, changing jobs, and critical illness are the top stressors in people's lives. Stress is detrimental to our well-being and clouds our ability to make wise decisions or think creatively.

There is no denying that going through the divorce process is difficult, but there are choices you can make to lessen the stress and turn this experience into a time of growth. The tools you use will be helpful with parenting and prove valuable in all areas of your life.

Choosing wisdom over anger and fear is a matter of connecting to a more positive, intuitive, and nurturing side of yourself. When we operate from wisdom, we open ourselves to possessing more peace, creativity, kindness, and a greater overall sense of wellness in our lives.

Attracting What You Feel

Statements made from fear and anger during a breakup often produce negative responses. It seems to be part of human nature. When someone sets a negative tone, it usually attracts a similar response. Take the examples below.

Anger	Angry Response
"You are a terrible mother."	*"We'll see about that in court."*
"If you don't pay your share of the baseball registration, you can't come to the games."	*"You can't stop me. I'll have my lawyer call your lawyer to be sure of that."*

To make things more difficult, fear-driven negotiations limit possibilities and solutions. Fear is a place where people become entrenched in their positions, gridlocked by senseless power struggles. Such power struggles make it difficult to negotiate with positive results.

Unfortunately, this often drives divorcing spouses into a court of law where they turn over the decision-making process to a judge. Courtroom divorces are often what we see in popular media such as movies and television, but handing your family's most important decisions over to a court of law often is not the best choice for you and your children. After all, who knows what's best for your children, you or the court?

Family courts are overcrowded with cases, limiting the time a judge or court mediator has to review each case. Unfortunately, the result can be that well-meaning attorneys who are trained to be adversarial are driving decisions about your children. Sometimes they do more harm than good. Even so, divorcing parents turn their cases and decisions over to the courts every day because they are polarized by fear and negative emotions.

If you and your co-parent can let go of negative emotions, you are best equipped to make decisions for your children and family—rather than a judge who has never met any of you. Family law judges and court mediators work hard to be fair. But the people who know your children best are you and your co-parent. By keeping the decision-making process between the parents, you will ensure your children's best interests.

When parents need help determining the best parent plan, there are better resources available than the courts for parents who are open and willing to work together. Those resources include mediators, child specialists, collaborative attorneys, and co-parent coordinators.

Tools for Managing Emotions

There are many tools available to help you manage and even triumph over whatever emotions might be working against your desire to be a better parent and a more effective person. Below are some tools I recommend that are healthy and can help you release negative emotions caused by stress.

Even if some of them are new to you, I encourage you to try them.

Releasing Emotions through Movement

Movement can help you release intense emotions. Exercise and movement will not only help you feel good, it has a side benefit of helping you look good too. When we hear the word "exercise" we often think of it as another task we have to do. But let's look at exercise in a new way. Think of it as "movement."

When we experience conflict or stress, we often hold tension in our bodies. Movement releases natural chemicals in our brains that improve our moods. Through movement, you can move out of stress and into a more positive state of mind.

To a busy single parent, adding one more thing to do may seem overwhelming, but movement does not have to add to your list of "have to do's." Movement can become a way of life. When you get up in the morning, start by taking a few minutes to wake up your body by stretching. You do not have to attend a yoga class to do yoga stretches.

Think of parking in a new way. Look for a parking spot that is a distance from the store so that you and your children can have the benefit of doing some extra walking. Or better yet, walk or ride your bike to the store.

Incorporate movement into your parenting. Children can benefit emotionally from movement. Make movement a family affair. Turn off the television, turn on the music and dance together. Singing also involves movement, so take time to sing with your children. Music is a wonderful way to increase your desire for movement and has proven beneficial effects on the brain.

Take up a family sport together. The possibilities are endless: bicycling, hiking, swimming, bowling, walking, rollerblading, skiing, or tennis. Join a gym. It's a great place for families. Most gyms and health clubs have programs for children too.

One of my clients took up tennis the year she and her ex separated and was amazed at how much negative energy she got rid of on the tennis court. Little things that used to break her in the early months of the separation hardly got to her at all once she got involved in the running, serving, reaching, swinging movements of tennis. Before taking up tennis, she sometimes yelled at her teenagers when they drove her crazy. Now she approaches things more calmly.

Find the movement that fits your body and lifestyle and notice the positive change in your emotions.

Mindfulness and Meditation

Meditation can help you deal with stress. Meditation and mindfulness have been proven to reduce stress in studies conducted at the University of Massachusetts Medical School and other places.

The art of meditation has been practiced for centuries. Meditation can lead you to being more mindful. Mindfulness is learning to slow down, pay attention, and become aware, all of which will help you deal with stress. Mindfulness meditation works best when you take time each day to slow down and sit alone quietly. The goal during this time is to recognize your thoughts *as just thoughts*. As you sit in meditation, rest in a larger awareness that is healing and restorative. Yes, there may be huge waves of emotion associated with your thoughts. Still, you can train yourself to remember to let these thoughts register in your awareness *as emotions* without either suppressing them or getting more inflamed by them. It helps to stay connected to an awareness of your body and ground yourself in your breathing when things are most tumultuous.

While this approach sounds simple, it is not that easy and requires a certain kind of discipline and self-compassion. As human beings we habitually busy our minds. This has increased our stress, added to personal conflict, and reduced our ability to creatively solve problems. By taking time for mindfulness meditation and bringing it into our daily lives, we create a greater opportunity to find solutions to our daily problems and to live a more peaceful life.

To learn more about mindfulness meditation, we recommend books and courses by Jon Kabat-Zinn, the founder of the Mindfulness Based Stress Reduction Program at the University of Massachusetts. He has spent more than thirty years studying the effects of meditation.

For more information on mindfulness meditation, refer to the Resources section on our website, collaborativecoparenting.com.

Eating Healthy Food

"You are what you eat." We have been told what we should eat, but we don't always do it. We need motivation. Right now, your motivation for eating healthy food is your own well-being. Eating well will help you obtain the energy you need as a single parent. It is also an opportunity to be a good role model for your children.

As Dr. Michael F. Roizen and Dr. Mehmet C. Oz write in *You On A Diet*, "Eating right shouldn't be about feeling bad. It should be about feeling strong, increasing energy, living better, feeling healthier, and having more fun than a front-row rock fan."

The *You* books by Dr. Roizen and Dr. Oz can help you understand your biology, deal with any physical challenges you face, and get the most out of your body. If you have health issues, talk to a licensed nutritionist or a doctor about changing your diet for the better.

A "Brain Healthy" Diet

In addition to affecting your physical health, food can affect your moods and emotions. Dr. Daniel Amen, a psychiatrist and nationally recognized expert on the relationship between the brain and behavior, recommends a "brain healthy" diet.

This includes protein, such as turkey or chicken, whole grains, green leafy vegetables, and healthy fats that contain omega three fatty acids, which are found in tuna, salmon, avocados, walnuts, and other foods. Dr. Amen writes, "Since the brain is 85% water, anything that dehydrates you is bad for the brain, such as alcohol, caffeine, excess salt, or not drinking enough fluids."

Dr. Amen urges patients to stop poisoning their brains: "Do not put toxic substances in your body. If you poison your brain you poison your mind."

Counseling

Sometimes you can't solve a problem on your own. You may need someone with special training and experience to help you manage emotions during this difficult time. Some of these professionals are listed below.

• **Licensed mental health professionals.** Mental health services are provided by several different professions, each of which has its own training and areas of expertise. Finding the right professional for you or a loved one can be a critical ingredient in the process of diagnosis, treatment, and recovery in the face of life's challenges. It's best to seek a referral. You can ask a family law attorney, a friend, or a family member.

Here are some of your options:

- o **Licensed Marriage Family Therapists** have master's degrees in psychology, counseling, or a similar discipline and have post-graduate experience. They may provide services that include diagnosis and counseling (individual, family/group or both). They have a license issued in their state.

- o **Licensed Social Workers** have master's degrees and post-graduate experience. Social workers provide various services including assessment and treatment of mental illnesses and psychotherapy.

- o **Licensed Psychologists** have doctoral degrees in clinical, educational, counseling, or research psychology. They can provide psychological testing and evaluations, treat emotional and behavioral problems and mental disorders, and provide psychotherapy.

- **Some of these licensed mental health professionals** specialize in child custody and divorce matters. They include:

  - o **Child specialists,** who help children express their feelings and reactions to the divorce and family issues. The child specialists then use this information to help parents better understand their children and meet their needs.

  - o **Divorce coaches,** who teach skills—such as anger management and communication—that help divorcing spouses reach agreement.

  - o **Private confidential mediators,** who are neutral parties that sit down with both divorcing spouses—at the same time—and help them make informed choices regarding their parenting plan and other matters related to divorce.

Understanding Fear

How do fear and wisdom affect our emotions and behavior? Fear makes us anxious about a possible situation or event. Wisdom grounds our emotions and helps us make healthy decisions.

Fear and wisdom bring opposite results. Being fearful paralyzes our ability to make wise decisions. Fear makes us anxious and paranoid. When we choose wisdom over fear, we make choices from a reasonable, constructive foundation.

Divorce can generate a great deal of fear. Fear often creates an inaccurate picture of how bad things really are. Wisdom, on the other hand, allows us to think clearly about a situation. The power of wisdom is available to everyone.

When we live in fear, we tend to act out with anger, abuse, guilt, competition, defensiveness, insecurity, lack, pain, and sickness. To make matters worse, fear breeds fear. The more we act out the emotion, the more fearful or angry we become. By focusing on fearful thoughts, we sometimes attract the very thing we dread.

How Fear Progresses

- Given a breeding place in our minds, it will fill the whole body.
- Once in the body, it generates an emotional fever, keeping us from our innate wisdom.
- Fear can eat away at our spirit and block the forward path of our actions.
- Fear is the greatest enemy of progress. Progress moves forward. In contrast, fear makes us consumed with the smallest aspects of our past pain and prevents our moving forward.

Are You Operating from Fear or Wisdom?

Learning to understand what we feel and owning our own emotions is the key to shifting from a place of fear to a place of wisdom. But how will you know whether you're operating from wisdom or fear?

When you think you might be operating from fear, give yourself the following test. If you answer "yes" to any of these questions, you are probably operating from a place of fear.

- Are you feeling vengeful?
- Are you feeling defensive?
- Are you feeling anxious?
- Are you feeling like a victim?
- Are you feeling paralyzed and unable to make decisions?

How to Know When You're Operating from Wisdom

To open up to the wisdom inside, we must be willing to listen to all points of view. Wisdom requires that we stop making up our minds in advance about how things should be, and that we learn to stop believing there is only one way to do things. Here are some questions you can ask yourself to be sure you're operating from wisdom:

- Are you feeling open to new ideas?
- Are you able to let go of knowing exactly what the outcome should be?
- Are you able to focus on the benefits for all, not focusing solely on what *you* want?
- Are you feeling a sense of emotional balance?
- Are you feeling hopeful?

~ EXERCISE ~

Fear vs. Wisdom

Name a time in your relationship breakup where fear blinded you from the truth.

_____

_____

_____

_____

Name a time when fear made a conflict worse.

_____

_____

_____

_____

How could this have been different had you operated from wisdom?

_____

_____

_____

_____

Think of at least one parenting decision you made based in wisdom rather than fear and write how it made you feel.

_____

_____

_____

Am I in This Alone?

Maybe you want to bring more wisdom into your life, but you think your co-parent is not capable of making decisions with a collaborative spirit. Don't underestimate the power of leading by example. Trust that your positive example will create the desired results. We'll discuss how to deal with very difficult and uncooperative co-parents later, but for now you are the one who is ready for change. During this process, your wisdom will benefit your children, yourself, and your co-parent too.

"Anger is often due to feeling powerless."
– John O'Neal, MD

Anger: A Fear-Based Emotion

Anger is a fear-based emotion that brings about conflict. When we are fearful or feel powerless, we often get angry.

Dealing with the fear and anger that can result from divorce can be challenging. However, if you can stop long enough to see how fearful emotions affect the choices you make, you have a greater chance of moving forward in peace.

One helpful exercise is to begin by seeing that *you are not your anger.* Those feelings are not you—they are an emotion. One way to externalize fear-driven hostility is to put that emotion outside yourself. At first, it may be difficult to see the emotions as separate from yourself, but once you are able to externalize your anger, you will take power over it, rather than it having power over you. I will show you how to do this in the next section.

A Conversation with Anger

To externalize an emotion, try having a conversation with it, as if the emotion could stand beside you and talk. To better understand this process, let's observe Lia, who was often angry in her marriage. Lia wanted to get to the root of her anger, so her divorce coach asked her to have a conversation with her anger. It went like this:

Lia: Why are you here, Anger?

Anger: I want to protect you, Lia.

Lia: What are you protecting me from?

Anger: People who hurt you, like Matt. I don't trust your ex.

Lia: Why are you so angry with him?

Anger: Because he only listens to you when you get angry—the same with the children.

Lia: Why and when did we start doing this?

Anger: When your father wouldn't listen to you when you were a child. You got angry and it got his attention. Remember, Lia?

Lia: Hmmmm. My mother did the same thing. She raised her voice to get his attention.

Anger: See, I am useful to you. People listen to you when I am around and you feel heard and powerful.

Lia: I want you to go away, Anger.

Anger: What? But you need me. How will you get attention from others?

Lia: I want to learn new, better ways to communicate. You have caused a lot of harm in my relationships. Anger, I want you to go away.

Anger: Not so fast; I've been around a long time.

Lia: Yes, it will take work, but I can do it. You're an emotion. You are NOT WHO I AM.

In talking to her anger, Lia learned why she thought anger had value and the origin of this strong emotion in her personality. This allowed her to gain some distance from that emotion. Lia worked hard to see her hostility as being outside herself. During this process, she became much better at externalizing and controlling her anger.

> *"Wisdom is to the mind*
> *what health is to the body."*
> *~ Francois de la Rochefoucauld*

The Physical Effects of Anger and Fear

When you are angry at someone, it is actually more harmful to you than it is to the other person. How does your body feel when you're afraid or angry? How well do you sleep, eat, and concentrate?

Your thoughts and emotions exert enormous power. When you become aware of how emotions affect your body and that you actually have control over those feelings, you can move toward taking apart or "deconstructing" the negative emotions that do not benefit you.

Let's do an exercise that will help you understand this principle:

• Think of someone you love who brings you an inner smile. Maybe it's your best friend who always stands by you. Maybe it's that hairdresser who makes you laugh, or that creative cousin who has such an upbeat attitude. Or maybe it's your grandmother because she always sees the best in you.

~ EXERCISE ~

Write down the name of the person you are thinking of:

_____

• Now focus on the emotions and sensations associated with this person. Allow no other thoughts except pleasant inner gratitude about this individual to enter your mind.

Write how this made you feel, including any physical sensations.

_____

_____

_____

• Chances are you feel joy, peacefulness, safety, and a flowing sense of connection to this person. This state of emotion allows you to be a more creative, kind, loving person and parent.

Now let's try something different:

• Think of someone who makes you feel angry or afraid.

Write this person's name: _____

• Now focus on the emotions and sensations associated with this person. Allow no other thoughts except anger and fear about this individual to enter your mind.

Write how this made you feel, including any physical sensations.

_____

_____

_____

• Chances are you felt tense, shut down, restricted, and less open.

This state of emotion keeps us from experiencing our best self and can affect our health. When we experience limiting emotions, we are unable to reach our full, healthy potential as creative and productive people and parents.

Depression

The emotional and physical loss of a relationship can bring on depression. In fact, depression is more likely during divorce or during a relationship breakup than at most other times. This is caused by both mental and physical changes.

Managing depression is critical at a time when so many decisions need to be made. If there are any thoughts of harming yourself or others, the depression needs to be managed through medical treatment. If the depression is mild, taking care of yourself through exercise, diet, and meditation will be helpful. Finding a support group can help as well. Search online for organizations that can refer you to professionals who can help with depression. If depression interferes with your daily functioning, it is of utmost importance to you and your children that you reach out and get help.

Trying Times, Wisdom, and Your Children

Remember that you are a role model for your children. The example you live teaches your children how to deal with everyday challenges, including when strong emotions threaten to undo you. What you can teach them during the most difficult times is that all situations, no matter how difficult, offer us opportunities to learn and grow.

The greatest gift we can offer our children is a hopeful outlook on life, no matter what our circumstances may be. Choosing wisdom over fear allows us to make positive choices for our children. If you feel fearful, chances are your children will feel the same. If you have an optimistic, courageous attitude, your children will be influenced positively as they learn healthy skills from your example.

Of course, growing through divorce or a breakup is not easy. Personal development takes patience, determination, and emotional awareness. Your desire for wholeness ultimately will draw you toward the inner wisdom you seek. Use the motivation of giving the gift of well-being to your children to propel you forward each and every day.

Goals

In order to keep life from just happening to you, it's important to set both long-term and short-term goals. Long-term goals are your desires for the future. They help you focus on how life *can* be. These goals might be one, two, or even five years away. Short-term goals are the stepping stones you use to reach your long-term goals. Here are a few examples of long-term co-parenting goals and the short-term goals that would lead to them.

Long-term goal: I will remain calm and focused when meeting with my co-parent.

Related short-term goals:

- Before talking to my co-parent, I will take a brief break and calm myself.
- I will create a support system for myself in order to deal with stress. It will include regular exercise and therapy.

Long-term goal: I will respect my co-parent's right to parent differently.
Related short-term goals:

- I will not ask my children unnecessary questions about their time with their other parent.
- Unless my child is in danger, I will not be too picky, critical, or demanding of my co-parent.

Long-term goal: I will support my children's relationship with their other parent.
Related short-term goals:

- I will be consistent in maintaining our co-parent plan.
- I will not schedule activities with my children that will conflict with my co-parent's time.

It's Important to Write Down Your Goals
It's one thing to have goals in your head, but writing them down gives them power. Why?

- Writing your goals makes them feel real.
- Writing your goals keeps them in the forefront of your mind.
- Writing your goals helps you realize they are attainable.

• I learned early in my life that writing down my goals was almost a magic way to achieve success. When I put my goals in writing, they seem to happen more easily. In mediation, I help my clients write down their goals. They tell me it helps them clarify the direction they want to go, stay focused, and ultimately achieve their goals.

~ EXERCISE ~

Create an Action Plan

You can start achieving your goals today. Begin by writing down one goal you'd like to achieve in your co-parenting relationship. List the short-term goals that will lead you there.

LONG-TERM CO-PARENTING GOAL

_____

_____

_____

SHORT-TERM CO-PARENTING GOAL
#1 _____

SHORT-TERM CO-PARENTING GOAL
#2 _____

Procrastination

We may find ourselves procrastinating and unable to set goals. Sometimes we are overwhelmed by our lives. Other times we are paralyzed by perfectionism and fear we won't measure up. And sometimes we feel resentful because we are being forced to do things against our will, such as comply with court orders.

If you find yourself procrastinating, try setting small goals. Focus on accomplishing a little each day. Don't be hard on yourself. Remember that you don't have to arrive at your long-term goals overnight. That's what short-term goals are for. There's no need to feel overwhelmed. Just take it one baby step at a time.

"When one door closes, another opens."
~ Alexander Graham Bell, inventor

Be Willing to Change Direction

Never be so set on a particular path that you can't change direction when circumstances change. I learned to set goals from my dad, who had a natural ability to get things done. When I was twenty, my father and I set a goal to acquire investment houses together. Unfortunately, not long after setting this goal, my father died.

His sudden death propelled me to focus on the goals we'd set together. Over the next few years, it became my passion to acquire houses. Despite my youth, the miraculous power of goal setting motivated me to buy several houses in just five years.

Later, the man who would become my husband and my daughter's father suggested I reevaluate my goal. Since the houses all had mortgages and I had an ongoing negative cash flow, he wisely recommended that I focus less on the number of houses I owned and more on my cash flow. Over the years, this proved to be a better approach. I learned that it's wiser to change a goal than stick to something that isn't working.

Visualizing

Sometimes it helps to visualize your goals. Two superstar golfers, Jack Nicklaus and Tiger Woods, use visualization to prepare and win at golf. Woods visualizes exactly where he wants the ball to go. These athletes are by no means alone. In 1998, baseball player Mark McGwire told *The New York Times* he broke the single-season home run record using visualization techniques. Olympic track-and-field champion Carl Lewis won his ten medals, nine of them gold, by envisioning himself winning the races in advance of the actual contests.

Visualization has helped me too. I had a goal to write a book on co-parenting, but I had a difficult time getting this book into form. Then, one afternoon, I sat down quietly to visualize how this book would look. I imagined the chapters and even saw the title. I watched the chapters unfold in my mind. Afterward I took time to write down the outline of what I had visualized. Then I began filling in more detail. I became motivated by my vision. I saw how my book could make a difference in the lives of divorcing parents and their children. This kept me going.

Of course, visualizing alone didn't write this book. I had to do my part. After visualization, there is always work to be done.

For me, it took a written goal, visualization, and action to write this book.

A Positive Co-Parent Visualization

Choose a future family event. It might be a holiday celebration, your child's graduation, or the birth of your first grandchild. Visualize a positive outcome for the family event.

REVIEW OF WEEK 4

- Eating well will help you obtain the energy you need as a single parent. It is also an opportunity to be a good role model for your children.
- Acting on intense emotions is often a mistake because:
  - Intense emotions frequently tell stories that aren't true.
  - Emotions come and go, but actions have consequences.
  - It's better to cool down and act on the basis of what's true.
- When we operate from fear, we tend to experience more anger, abuse, pain, and sickness—and we often attract the very thing we dread.
- When you are angry at your co-parent, it is more harmful to you than to them.
- If you have an optimistic, courageous attitude, your children will be influenced positively as they learn healthy skills from your example.
- Long-term goals are your desires for the future. They help you focus on how life *can* be. These goals might be one, two, or even five years away.
- Short-term goals are stepping stones that help you reach long-term goals.

- Writing down your goals makes them feel real, keeps them in the forefront of your mind, and helps you realize they are attainable.
- Sometimes we procrastinate after setting goals because we are overwhelmed by the sheer size of our goals, we fear we can't achieve our goals, or we resent having to achieve goals we didn't freely choose.
- Visualization helps you define what you want the future to look like.
- When we operate from wisdom, we open ourselves to more peace, creativity, and kindness.
- Fear-driven negotiations create conflict, limit possibilities and solutions, and make people defensive.
- Tools for dealing with the stress of divorce include movement and exercise, meditation, and eating healthy food.
- The emotional and physical loss of a relationship can bring on depression.
- To determine whether you're operating from fear or wisdom, ask yourself: Am I feeling angry? Am I feeling defensive? Am I feeling anxious?
- When you are operating from a place of wisdom, you will be open to new ideas, seek to benefit everyone involved (not just yourself), and be optimistic.

WEEK 4 ACTION ITEMS

- Complete the exercises in Week 4.
- Use the "Tools for Managing Emotions" in this chapter and journal about how these tools worked for you.

WEEK 5, APPRECIATING DIFFERENCES

What You Will Find in Week 5:

• Knowing Yourself
• The DISC Assessment
• Appreciating Different Parenting Styles
• Gender Differences
• Money Differences
• Religious Differences
• Respecting Differences

"Always remember that you are absolutely unique. Just like everybody else."
~ *Margaret Mead, anthropologist*

KNOWING YOURSELF

Because no two people are alike, it stands to reason that no two parents are exactly alike either. Each of us has a unique personality that makes our parenting style different from other people's styles.

Not realizing this leads many parents into conflict because they tend to expect the other parent to parent the same way they do. This kind of thinking is common but very unrealistic. There are many ways to parent children. Getting away from thinking there is only one way will help your co-parenting relationship.

Before we look more deeply into this idea, let's take some time for you to get to know yourself better. Before you can assess your interactions with others, including your co-parent, it's important to understand your own behaviors and personality first.

The personal assessment we'll use here is an abbreviated version of DISC, one of the oldest, most validated assessments in the training, leadership, and self-awareness fields. DISC is used to improve relationships, teamwork, communication, and work productivity while minimizing stress and conflict.

The foundation for DISC was first explained by an early inventor of the lie detector, William Moulton Marston, in his book *Emotions of Normal People* (1928). He believed that every person has a behavioral style—a predictable pattern of behavior and emotions. This style consists of how a person acts, how an individual sees the world, and how a person feels.

Many companies have since developed Marston's ideas into assessment tests that help employers understand the strengths and weaknesses of employees. Individuals use DISC to understand themselves and how they interact with others.

DISC assessments can help you:

• Understand your behavior and how it affects others
• Adapt your behavior to get more positive results
• Examine your reactions to other people's behavior
• Develop a positive attitude about yourself through improved self-awareness

> *"First, know thyself."*
> *~ Socrates, Greek philosopher*

By knowing yourself better, you will improve your ability to communicate with others. This will help you form better relationships with your co-parent and others.

The DISC Assessment

The four dimensions in the DISC grid represent certain aspects of the personality—whether you are faster-paced or slower-paced and task-focused or people-focused.

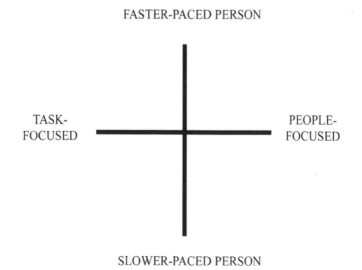

~ EXERCISE ~

Your DISC Assessment

On the grid above and using the vertical (up and down) line, place a dot on the line indicating whether you are a FASTER-PACED PERSON or a SLOWER-PACED PERSON. If you are very fast-paced, for instance, your dot will be at the top of the line.

Then place a dot on the horizontal line indicating whether you are more task-focused or people-focused. Connect the two dots and shade in the triangle.

Your triangle will be located in one of the four corners on the chart above. Now look at the following chart to learn more about your personality traits.

FASTER-PACED PERSON

* Direct * Motivated by Results * Accepts Challenges * Good Leader * Makes Decisions Quickly * Likes Prestige	* Interactive * Enthusiastic * Good Communicator * Influential * Friendly * Not Good with Deadlines

TASK-FOCUSED   **D** | **I**   PEOPLE-FOCUSED

C | **S**

* Conscientious * Analytical * Systematic * Detail-oriented * Good Planner * Critical * Makes Decisions Slowly * Reserved	* Steady * Patient * Slow to Change * Calms Excited People * Predictable * Accommodator

SLOWER-PACED PERSON

Now that you've done the exercise and read the tendencies above, you know a little more about yourself. The next step is to understand how this relates to your interactions with others.

Go back to the DISC grid and find out which behavior style best describes your co-parent. Then read the charts below. Take a moment to see how you and your co-parent have unique behaviors or, if you are similar, what challenges that presents.

D

D characteristics	Direct, decisive, problem solver, risk taker
D's fear...	Being taken advantage of
D's want...	Authority, prestige, freedom, variety in life
With a D, do...	Be brief, solve problems, highlight logical benefits of ideas
With a D, don't...	Ramble, make generalizations, make statements without support
D's should learn to...	Be active listeners, value others' ideas and feelings, be less domineering

I

I characteristics	Interactive, enthusiastic, optimistic, trusting, emotional, persuasive
I's fear...	Rejection
I's want...	Acceptance, friends, recognition, positive working relationship
With an I, do...	Build a friendly, favorable environment; let them talk about ideas, people, and their intuition; create incentives

With an I, don't...	Eliminate social time, do all the talking, ignore their ideas or accomplishments, tell them what to do
I's should learn to...	To be less impulsive, focus more on facts, talk less, listen more. Follow through on tasks

S

S characteristics	<u>Steady</u>, good listener, friendly, predictable
S's fear...	Loss of security
S's want...	Security, time to adjust to change, limited area of responsibility, few conflicts or surprises
With an S, do...	Create a comfortable environment, provide clarification, present ideas in a non-threatening manner, explain how change will minimize risk
With an S, don't...	Be pushy, overly aggressive or demanding. Don't be confrontational
S's should learn to...	Be more open to change, focus on goals rather than procedure, work at expressing thoughts, ideas, and feelings

C

C characteristics	<u>Conscientious</u>, accurate, careful, fact-finder, high standards
C's fear...	Criticism
C's want...	Reassurance, precise expectations and goals, planned change, independence

With a C, do…	Prepare ideas in advance, delineate pros and cons, be patient and diplomatic
With a C, don't…	Refuse to discuss details, answer questions casually or vaguely, make differences personal
C's should learn to…	Be less critical of others' ideas and methods, be more decisive, focus less on facts and more on people, and build relationships.

~ EXERCISE ~

What Did You Learn?
What did you learn about yourself?

_____

_____

What did you learn about others?

_____

_____

What will you do differently now that you have this information?

_____

_____

Appreciating Differences

As you were learning more about yourself and your co-parent through the DISC assessment, you likely thought about the ways your co-parent is different from you. It's important to remember that different is not better or worse. Different styles bring unique gifts, talents, and wisdom into our children's lives, but no single personality style is more important than another.

You naturally feel more comfortable if your children receive one style of parenting—yours. While this may be a reflection of our natural desire to control, try keeping an open mind about the benefit of differences.

If your co-parent spoke French to your children while you spoke Spanish, would one language be better than the other? Your children would learn the languages of both parents.

In the same respect, try thinking of your individual styles as an opportunity for your children to become *socially* bilingual while interacting in real world situations.

Respect for differences also is a gift you can give your children. When parents have different styles—and they often do—valuing your co-parent's gifts and uniqueness is a way of honoring each child's whole being.

In school, for example, some teachers appreciate a child's creativity in the classroom while others want strict order. As long as what the teacher asks isn't extreme, children usually learn "how it is" in each classroom and adjust to that environment.

If your children are exposed to different personality styles, it will be easier to adapt to diverse personalities as they grow.

What Style of Parent Are You?

Now that you know more about yourself and your co-parent, look at the chart below to learn how these styles might influence parenting.

Start with the "description" box. The description should align with the traits listed alongside the letter you came up with in the DISC exercise.

Parenting styles each have value. Look at the styles in the chart below and notice how interesting it is that each style has its own strengths and weaknesses.

STYLES	DESCRIPTION	POSITIVES	POSSIBLE PROBLEM AREAS
D	Parents who love being in charge. They are leaders, activators, and organizers. They are protective of the family unit, want to provide financially, offer guidance to the children, and provide good role models of leadership qualities.	D's get things done. They do it all with self-confidence. They like challenges and leading others.	They often fail to delegate, do too much, and don't let others participate. They can be insensitive.
I	Parents who are social, outgoing, optimistic, and like to organize group activities. They create special family time, hug children frequently, and encourage children to explore the world.	I's are team players and "people" people who like energizing and entertaining others.	They have difficulty setting priorities and meeting deadlines, are easily distracted, and fear loss of social approval.
S	Parents who are tolerant, devoted, adaptable, polite, and respectful. They take time with their children, and don't anger easily when things go wrong.	S's are stable, dependable, and easy-going. They enjoy creating comfort zones for everyone around them.	They can have problems taking a stand and say "yes" when they want to say "no." They have trouble setting boundaries and goals.

C	Parents who provide guidelines to help things run smoothly. They are detail-oriented. They encourage children to do well in school, keep the home orderly, and help children establish routines and set goals.	C's are systematic and organized. They weigh the pros and cons of a situation, and they value quality.	They tend to be perfectionists, worry a lot, and may have trouble trusting others.

~ EXERCISE ~

Based on the chart, what is your parenting personality, D, I, S or C?

_____

What are your strengths?

_____

_____

What are your weaknesses?

_____

_____

What are the strengths of your co-parent?

_____

_____

Think about how your parenting strengths complement those of your co-parent. What do your combined strengths model for your children?

_____

_____

_____

_____

Opposites

Have your ever heard the saying that "opposites attract"? It seems to be true in relationships. Many people choose a partner who is their opposite or who has qualities they find interesting, only to learn once they're married that the characteristics they fell in love with are now the very traits that drive them crazy. This can create problems when raising children. When you criticize your co-parent's personality and differences in front of your children, you are criticizing a part of them. Learning to embrace your co-parent's different style will help your children feel accepted.

The Extrovert and the Introvert

My co-parent, Art, is an introvert and I am an extrovert. This created some interesting situations as we raised our daughter together as co-parents.

When Jessica was young, I encouraged her to be as outgoing as possible. She and I often participated in activities with other families and children and we were very social.

In contrast, her father usually spent time alone with her when they were together. Their time was spent with just them, one-on-one, father and daughter.

The interesting thing is that our daughter, now in her twenties, is a little like both of us. She is outgoing and social, but she also often requests one-on-one time with people to allow for a more personal connection. She is at times an introvert and at other times an extrovert.

Did she learn to be focused and introverted from her father? Did she learn to be outgoing from me? I'm not sure. But what I can tell you is this: Jessica has personality qualities from both her mom and her dad. Knowingly or not, she has embraced parts of both of us.

Gender Differences

For many years, it was politically incorrect to suggest that gender differences existed. But thanks to the work of John Gray in his books *Men Are from Mars, Women Are from Venus* and the more recent *Why Mars & Venus Collide*, more people are grasping the fact that male and female brains are wired differently.

People's communication styles can vary drastically, whether due to gender, personality, culture, or other factors. Being aware of these differences can contribute to co-parenting success.

In my mediation practice, I often see gender differences, such as those that made problems for Andrew and Tina in the following story.

Andrew and Tina

Andrew and Tina were a divorcing couple who came to me to mediate an issue. Tina was worried that the children didn't seem to be getting enough sleep when they were at Andrew's house. As she went over her concerns, Andrew sat with his arms folded and his shoulder directed pointedly away from Tina.

When Tina had finished, I asked to hear Andrew's ideas and concerns about the children. Tina looked a little surprised. It appeared that Andrew had shut down and not offered suggestions in years.

Andrew, however, had perked up in his chair. I asked them to turn their chairs to face one another. Andrew talked about how his schedule with the children was so fragmented he had trouble sticking to a routine.

"Do you have any ideas for a change that would make your time with the children less fragmented?" I asked.

He suggested that changing his days with the children would work better with his schedule and give more consistency to the children's routines. Surprisingly, Tina chimed in that this proposed schedule worked better for her too.

"Why didn't you say something sooner?" she asked.

I knew the reason why. Andrew had retreated to his cave years before because he rarely felt listened to. Did he tell Tina? No. And she didn't zero in on the problem. It is important for both parents to keep the lines of communication open to effectively resolve challenges.

From that day on, we worked on new communication skills that acknowledged their different personality styles, putting them on the road to a more successful co-parenting partnership.

Money Differences

Money generates intense—and diverse—emotional responses. This is why money often causes bitter arguments between co-parents.

Some people view money with an attitude of abundance, creating a sense that "there will always be enough." Abundance-minded people enjoy their resources. However, that same attitude may lead individuals to become reckless with their spending: "I'll always have enough, so I'll buy the item now and figure out how to pay for it later."

The opposite view is one of scarcity or lack. These more thrifty people may be excellent savers. Their bank accounts may thrive while they prepare for a rainy day. On the negative side, those who feel a sense of scarcity about money may become misers, fearful of spending anything for pleasure at all.

Sometimes parents have the same approach to money—they spend too much. When this happens, there is no balance and the excess spending can create serious problems. This imbalance can create a distorted understanding about spending for your children.

Different responses to the same thing—money—makes getting along complicated. Ignoring those differences will lead to frustration. Being aware of your differences and understanding how your feelings about money might be different from those of your co-parent will help you work through child-related financial questions and challenges.

Religious Differences

Interfaith families have special challenges and special joys. On one hand, the children have a wealth of religions traditions and practices to draw from. On the other, the choice of celebrating two faiths can be a challenge requiring lots of give-and-take between the co-parents and the family as a whole. Learning to value differences can be extended to religious differences, even after a breakup or divorce.

Families that celebrate interfaith beliefs most successfully are often the ones that focus on the common themes in each faith instead of focusing on what makes the religions different. For instance, almost all religious holidays have some element of harmony, peace, and reconciliation in their traditions that can be celebrated in ways that send the same message to children about what the family values.

It is also my observation that when parents come from different religious practices and beliefs, children can benefit. Take for example Ricki and Dave, friends I have known for more than thirty years. Dave is Catholic and Ricki is Jewish. Over the last thirty years, this couple has nurtured a strong, happy marriage, raising two wonderful daughters while fully embracing their religious differences.

Although I've always been impressed by this couple's relationship, I was particularly struck one afternoon when I received a call from Dave inviting me to a Passover seder. Even though his wife and daughters were going out of town, Dave wanted to attend the celebration anyway, and Ricki encouraged Dave to invite me as his guest. I was honored to accept.

As the evening progressed, Dave shared that he and his family had been attending this Jewish celebration for more than twenty years. The tradition meant so much to Dave that even though his wife and daughters couldn't make it that night, he still didn't want to miss out on this annual ritual. When I asked him how his Catholic faith fit in, he explained that he gets plenty of opportunity to celebrate Easter and Christmas.

This family, with many traditions, has built one of the strongest networks of friends I have ever seen, and it's no wonder that Dave and Ricki's two daughters are such well-adjusted, happy young women. Rather than struggle with religious differences, their parents have chosen to respect and celebrate their differences.

Sometimes one parent is religious and the other parent is not. One of my clients wanted to pass on her Jewish faith to her son by sending him to Hebrew school. The boy's father wasn't religious, but he felt strongly about exposing their son to outdoor activities and nature. Each parent agreed to support the other as they involved their son in both these activities.

Respecting the Other Person's Parenting Style

There was a time when children who were born left-handed were encouraged to use their right hands instead because it was believed to be the "correct" choice. As you can imagine, this led to great difficulties in those children's ability to function, write, and do basic day-to-day activities. Just as being left-handed is natural for some and not inferior to being right-handed, one parenting style is not better than another style. They are simply different.

Children need both their parents' gifts. One parenting style is not more important than the other.

Recognizing the differences in personality styles between you and your co-parent and honoring the best of each style as it relates to parenting will benefit your children and provide you with a more respectful working relationship.

Valuing differences for the benefit of your children will also make you more flexible. Keep your children's best interests in the forefront of your mind and your feelings about your co-parent's differences will become less annoying.

Don't be too picky, critical or demanding when the real issue is simply that your co-parent's style is different from your own. Let small concerns or irritations pass. Instead, discuss major issues that concern your children's health, safety, education, and welfare.

Determine what is harmful to your children and what is just different. Pressuring or requesting one parent to adapt to the other parent's style may be invasive and could lead to unnecessary conflict. Asking people to change their style will result in resentment and a breakdown in the co-parent relationship. In addition, it sends a confusing message to the children, possibly making them doubt themselves or their parents.

Letting go of the frustration of differences can be very freeing. Finding the place where the differences can be complementary rather than conflicting is the goal of collaborative co-parenting.

"Nature arms each man with some faculty
which enables him to do easily
some feat impossible to any other."
~Ralph Waldo Emerson

~ EXERCISE ~

Benefits of Different Co-Parenting Styles

Write a brief description about how different co-parenting styles have benefited your children.

_____

_____

_____

_____

REVIEW OF WEEK 5

- Understanding your own personality can help you:
  - o Understand your behavior and how it affects others.
  - o Adapt your behavior to obtain more positive results.
  - o Develop a positive attitude about yourself.
- Personality styles fall into some general categories. They are called D, I, S, and C in the DISC system. Each style has its own strengths and weaknesses.
- The DISC chart tells you whether:
  - o You are a faster-paced or a slower-paced person.
  - o You are more task-focused or people-focused.
- The DISC evaluation can help you understand your own strengths and weaknesses—and work with your co-parent more successfully.
- Respect for differences is a gift you can give your children.
- One parenting style is not better than another. It's okay that children are exposed to more than one parenting style.
- When co-parenting, both men and women should try to appreciate and accommodate the other parent's communication style, which may be influenced by gender, personality, culture, or other factors.

- Co-parents must learn to respectfully discuss differences involving money, religion, and parenting styles.
- You should overlook small concerns and irritations involving your co-parent and discuss only those issues that affect your children's health, safety, education, and welfare.

WEEK 5 ACTION ITEMS

- Complete the exercises in Week 5.
- Observe the different personality styles of people around you.
- Journal about how your personality style does or does not work well with someone else's personality style.

WEEK 6, PARENTING TOOLS

What You Will Find in Week 6:

- Twelve Positive Discipline Parenting Tools
- Single Parenting
- Balancing Work, Parenting and Play
- Listening to Your Children
- Teamwork: Family Meetings
- Teaching Children About Money

TWELVE POSITIVE DISCIPLINE PARENTING TOOLS

The parenting skills in this program are based on positive discipline concepts. These concepts were originated by Alfred Adler, expanded by Rudolph Dreikurs, and put into easy-to-understand parent education principles by well-known author Jane Nelsen, a personal friend of mine.

For decades, Jane's *Positive Discipline* series has been the "how to" child-rearing book for many parents seeking kind-but-firm methods for raising responsible, respectful children, and I was fortunate to be Jane's co-author on one of the series' top-selling books, *Positive Discipline for Single Parents*.

The *Positive Discipline* series answers the age-old question of how to empower and encourage children to adopt appropriate behaviors without power struggles and resistance. What parent doesn't want this?

With that in mind, I am sharing some of the *Positive Discipline* principles with you because it's my experience that knowing these concepts will make your co-parenting challenges easier. For a deeper understanding and more information, I recommend that you read *Positive Discipline for Single Parents* and the other *Positive Discipline* books.

Let's dig in and take a look at these concepts.

PARENTING TOOL #1: BE KIND AND FIRM

Positive discipline is being kind and firm at the same time. Kindness shows respect for your children. Firmness shows respect for yourself. Setting limits with kindness and firmness provides a positive environment to solve parenting problems.

Take the common situation of homework. It is respectful and kind to involve your children in the decision of how and when the homework should be done. Being firm about the agreed time is respectful to all. Lecturing and yelling is not respectful to anyone. Children are much more willing to follow limits when they've been treated consistently and with respect.

PARENTING TOOL #2: CONNECTION BEFORE CORRECTION

It helps if your children know you're trying to see things from their point of view and that you understand their feelings. When your child won't pick up toys before bedtime, take a moment to get into your child's world and connect. You can say, "I know you're having fun and don't want to stop playing, but we have an agreement that eight o'clock is bedtime." Children will listen if they feel listened to and there is an understanding about limits.

PARENTING TOOL #3: LIMITED CHOICES

Offer your children at least two limited choices that you can live with. Do you want to do your homework before or after dinner? Do you want to hop like a bunny or slither like a snake while picking up your toys? Do you want pudding or an apple after eating your sandwich?

Make sure the choices are appropriate and acceptable. It is not appropriate to give them a choice about whether to brush their teeth or not or whether to go to bed when it's time. Acceptable means you can live with the choice they make. Respect whatever choices your children make when you give them several things to pick from. Offering choices helps your children learn to make decisions.

A friend often told her son to pick his toys up "anytime in the next ten minutes, your choice" and set a small timer in his room. That made him feel the timing for the chore was in his power.

PARENTING TOOL #4: CURIOSITY QUESTIONS

Ask "curiosity questions" to help children explore the consequences of their choices. When a child makes a mistake, ask questions rather than expressing your thoughts. "What did Jason do after you grabbed his scooter?" "How would you have felt if he took your scooter without asking?"

Too many parents tell children what happened, what caused it to happen, how they should feel, and what they should do. Telling discourages children from developing their own wisdom and from seeing mistakes as opportunities to learn.

PARENTING TOOL #5: REDIRECTION

Redirect children from inappropriate behavior to appropriate behavior. Here is one example of how redirection works:

While Jim was watching his son Joey play with a friend on the playground near their house, Jim noticed that Joey kept cutting in front of his friend. Jim got up, walked over to the boys, and gently moved Joey behind the other boy. "It's Sammy's turn first," he said. This is all that Jim needed to do to redirect Joey's behavior.

PARENTING TOOL #6: FOLLOW THROUGH

Decide what you will do and do it. Follow through instead of repeating yourself. One example of this is saying, "I will read you this story as soon as you've brushed your teeth." There is no need to say it over and over. Just wait until the child's teeth have been brushed before you read.

PARENTING TOOL #7: QUALITY TIME

Spend quality time with each child by staggering bedtimes or making sure there are certain days set aside for "special time"—like Tuesdays with Emily and Thursdays with Ryan. It only takes a small amount of time to truly connect with your children and make them feel special. This special time with each child can be outlined in your co-parent agreement.

PARENTING TOOL #8: EVERYONE IN ONE BOAT

In situations of minor conflict between your children, put them in the same boat. There's no reason to find out who started the problem or whose fault it is. Treating them the same and applying the same consequence will provide each child with the incentive to solve his or her own disputes in the future.

PARENTING TOOL #9:
POSITIVE TIME-OUT

Use positive time-outs to take children out of the moment of conflict so they can focus on solving the problem. This is a nurturing (not punitive) time. Think of a sports "time-out" that team members use to re-group, plan, or take a break. This is what your child needs: a break from negative behavior or time to get his or her emotions in order.

Positive time-outs are most effective when each child creates his or her own special place with whatever helps him or her "self-soothe," such as soft cushions, stuffed animals, books, or soft music. Then let children give their special place a name other than "time-out spot," such as "Emily's quiet place." This will help them remember that the purpose is to help them feel calm so they can feel better and access their "rational" brain.

PARENTING TOOL #10:
FAMILY MEETINGS

Hold family meetings regularly — and, yes, a single parent and even one child are still a family! The agenda for these meetings lets everyone be heard and is an opportunity to get everyone involved in problem solving. Family meetings are a wonderful occasion to create a team spirit.

PARENTING TOOL #11: TAKE TIME FOR TRAINING

Teach, with love, the skills needed to get the behavior you desire from your children. How can children know what's expected of them if you don't teach them first? Children want to learn and feel a sense of equality. Children learn from their mistakes. Let mistakes be teaching opportunities.

Teaching with love is not lecturing, but be sure that what you're asking is age appropriate. Young children, for instance, need help cleaning up messes in their room or they will get overwhelmed.

PARENTING TOOL #12: ALWAYS ENCOURAGE

Use encouragement instead of praise and rewards. Replace "I'm so proud of you" with "You must be so proud of yourself." This teaches children to find pride in themselves in a job well done rather than needing the approval and praise of others to feel accomplished.

> *"Children need encouragement like a plant needs water."*
> *~ Rudolph Dreikurs, child psychiatrist*

Single Parenting

As a single parent, your perception of your role has a great impact on your success. You need to decide whether challenges

117

are going to be opportunities to grow or whether obstacles will be treated like stumbling blocks.

If you face challenges with a healthy perspective, your children will notice your decision to face life with a positive attitude. Your children are likely to follow your lead because children like to mimic. Never forget that you are your children's most significant role model as they grow and mature.

How do you want your children to handle challenges and obstacles? What do you want to teach through your behavior? One of the greatest gifts you can give your children is a hopeful outlook on life no matter what the circumstances.

You are your children's teacher through your actions. Positive role modeling will not only benefit your children, it will also make your life easier.

Some single parents think they need to "make it up" to their children for not having two parents in the same home. They pamper their children, rescue them, and give them too many material things. This is a mistake that teaches children that love means getting others to take care of them and buy them things.

Part of good role modeling for your children includes getting a life of your own. Too many parents try to live through their children, wanting them to accomplish what they didn't or the same things they did. "Getting a life" means having your own hobbies or following your dreams while supporting your children in their dreams and aspirations. It does not mean neglecting your children, but if you are happy in your own life, this will reflect positively in theirs.

Balancing Single Parenting Work and Play

A balanced life is a joy to live. It may take some time to learn to juggle work, parenting, and a social life. But once you do, you will feel comfortable as a single parent.

The adjustment of returning to work and being a single parent was challenging for me because I had not had to support myself, let alone a child, for more than ten years. I learned to make my time count at work by becoming organized and by prioritizing.

It also was a challenge because my daughter wanted to be involved in everything: soccer, Girl Scouts, student body activities, and more. She loved parties and social gatherings. Keeping up with her schedule and getting her from place to place was like having a part-time job.

As a result of this, however, I became more organized. I was able to set priorities and actually became more efficient with my time as a single mom than I had been during my marriage. I became more efficient and was able to eliminate distractions more than ever before. I also noticed that I cherished the moments more when I took time to have fun on my own.

I learned early on that my best support system was my daughter's father. Although I did not relish his parenting skills at first, I did value the love he felt for our daughter and knew his intentions were always good. My daughter adores her daddy. It was the one place she could go and not miss her mommy too much. This allowed me to enjoy my time without her.

Listening to Your Children

Children need extra love, understanding, and attention during your separation and divorce. Careful listening with your head and your heart is one of the best ways a parent can connect with children. To truly hear what a child is saying, we must listen not only to the words, but to the tone, feelings, and body language.

One woman I know takes her young daughter's face lovingly in her hands and looks into her daughter's eyes when the child is trying to express something important. This gesture seems like a loving act directed toward the child, but the woman confided that it is just as much a reminder to herself to stop what she's doing and really listen.

In our busy lives, it's important to set aside or turn off distractions such as TVs, radios, and the newspaper as we listen to our children. What attitude do you adopt when your children try to talk to you? Does your body language or your facial expression say, "I'm busy," or "Not another problem!"—or do you seem open to whatever your children want to share?

Show you are listening by repeating back what your children say to you. Invite more discussion. Acknowledge your children's feelings.

Take a child who comes home from school upset about how the teacher got mad at him and all his classmates laughed. Would your first impulse be to ask what he did to make the teacher mad or to acknowledge his hurt feelings? A lecture can wait. First and foremost, children need to feel listened to and understood.

Listening: A Story

One day, a man came home from work to find his son waiting for him. "Daddy, can you stay home with me tomorrow?" the boy asked.

"Of course I can't stay home," the man answered. "If I don't go to work, I won't get paid. Now go play and let me rest. I'm very tired."

"Could you stay home if we had more money?" the boy asked.

The father grew impatient with the conversation. "It's late. Just go to bed."

The boy looked dejected as he headed off to his room.

During the evening, the father thought about the conversation and started to feel guilty. He looked into the boy's room and found that he was still awake. When the boy saw his father, he immediately sat up, smiled, and handed him something from the bedside table. It was his piggy bank.

"I'm giving you all my money so you don't have to go to work tomorrow," he said. "We can spend the whole day together."

The father's eyes welled up. All his son wanted was a little of his busy father's time.

How to Listen to Your Children

Pay attention. Watch for signs that your children need to talk. When you're listening, make sure you're giving 100 percent of your attention to your children.

Make eye contact.

Be specific when you ask questions. Say, "What games did you play at recess today?" rather than "How was school?" This shows your child that you're interested.

Use an echo to show your children you're listening. "So, what I hear you saying is that Tom got mad at you today and you're not sure why."

Shutting Down Communication

Parents sometimes are unaware that certain words and phrases hurt attempts to communicate openly with a child. Be aware of what you say and how you say it. Here are some phrases that break down communication.

- *Blaming: "Why don't you ever..."*
- *Preaching: "I've told you time and time again..."*
- *Threatening: "If you don't do what I tell you, I'll..."*
- *Intimidating: "Because I said so."*
- *Putting Down: "You think you're so smart" or "You don't know anything."*

Give hugs and kisses. Children of all ages need physical affection, especially when they need comforting.

Schedule plenty of one-on-one time with your children. This can be fun time, but it also can be working side by side doing chores as long as you're talking, sharing, and learning about one another.

Listen to your children without judgment. This lets your children know that their feelings, thoughts, and values are valid, important, and have meaning.

Teamwork: Family Meetings

Family meetings are special times when you gather together to solve problems, set goals, appreciate one another and to build a team spirit. Yes, single-parent families are families too—and family meetings are an opportunity to remind your children of that. The size of your family does not matter. Even if you have only one child, family meetings will strengthen your team.

How to Conduct Family Meetings

Families are unique, so each family's meeting will differ in many ways. Here are some guidelines and tips that might help you plan yours:

- **Set Aside Time Each Week**—Setting the family meeting at a regular time each week and making it a priority will make it a tradition and support its success.
- **Appreciations and Compliments**—Start the family meeting each week with sharing appreciations and compliments. During the week, look for actions or accomplishments that you can comment on at the beginning of the meeting.

- **Agenda Board**—Keep an agenda board in a handy place and encourage family members to add things to the agenda for the meeting all week. No idea is a bad idea.
- **Everyone Gets Involved**—Decide who will lead the meeting. Choose a secretary. Getting everyone involved creates a more committed team and makes for a better meeting.
- **Write It Down**—Have a white board at the meeting so that you can write down any problems or solutions. Working on solving problems together will allow for more solutions. Often children will come up with ideas about how to solve a challenge that you would not have come up with on your own. Let every idea be a possibility. Create an atmosphere of cooperation. Children tend to accept solutions they helped come up with.
- **Enjoy Your Time Together**—A tradition of family meetings can become the foundation of special moments together and cherished memories of how your family worked out problems or listened to one another. This also is where your children learn that their thoughts, feelings, and ideas are listened to and taken seriously.
- **End with a Celebration**—At the end of the meeting have a treat, a song, a prayer, or some fun activity you all enjoy doing together. Anything that celebrates working together will do.

The Benefits of Family Meetings

Regular family meetings accomplish many positive goals. Family meetings are a commitment to your family. Often we commit to get-togethers with our friends and co-workers or professional or social groups, but what about making "appointments" with our children?

Solving problems together also creates the opportunity to build mutual respect. Taking time for conversation and understanding one another's point of view deepens the life-bond of the family. Children should be given the opportunity to problem-solve and be listened to at family meetings. This promotes self-confidence and gives them skills that last children a lifetime.

Creating a tradition of family meetings also can be a foundation for special memories together.

Children and Money Management

One reality of being a single parent is that there is less income than before. As a result, money management is necessary. Getting the children involved in budgeting can be an enriching opportunity as long as you don't get them caught up in your financial worries. Children can begin learning money management as early as they have the developmental skill to count.

Children's Basic Money-Management Principles

- *Allowances: Decisions to make before setting your children's allowance include the proper age-appropriate amount, conditions (such as doing chores for the allowance or not), and financial goals or agreements about savings, charitable contributions, or spending.*
- *Budgeting: Budgeting is a great opportunity to learn financial responsibility. Some things children can budget for include eating out, special clothes, sports, school supplies, party expenditures, gifts, extra-curricular activities, books, toys, and games.*
- *Savings: Even if it is as small as pennies in a piggy bank or a small savings account at your local bank, saving money teaches children fiscal responsibility.*

How does money management work in real family scenarios? Let me tell you about Rick. He was a single parent with three growing children who had all acquired expensive tastes during the marriage. After the divorce, the family had limited money, and Rick found himself in frustrating power struggles over the children's desire to spend money.

Rick and the children decided upon a monthly allowance. The children loved the idea that they would have their own money. Teaching the children to budget with their own money restored the family's balance of power. The children no longer continually harassed their father about buying things. Instead, they weighed the importance of an item against their needs, desires, and budget. The agreement relieved stress, diminished resentment, decreased costs, and reduced competition among the siblings. It also helped the children learn to handle money more responsibly.

Take one or two parenting tools you have learned in this chapter and start applying them now. Be kind to yourself. Changes come in baby steps.

~ EXERCISE ~

Personal Timeline

The personal timeline you're about to draw can help children feel more settled about the future. Put each child's name above the word "birth." The off-center line is called "divorce." Fill in significant events between the two lines such as the birth of a sibling, starting school, new pets, an especially fun vacation, and other positive things from your child's life. Put in a few "bad" things, too, such as the death of a pet or a time your child was sad.

Now put in future events to the right of "divorce" on the timeline that you know your child is looking forward to, or good things you can predict will happen in the future.

This shows your children that many things happen in life—some bad, many good. Events such as divorce can be tough, but there are many good times ahead. Be sure to share this timeline with each child, working through filling it out together.

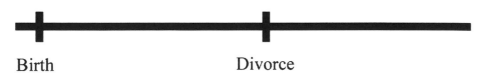

Birth   Divorce

REVIEW OF WEEK 6

• Positive discipline involves being kind and firm at the same time.

- Connecting before correcting helps children feel understood and listened to.
- When you offer children choices, all the choices should be appropriate and acceptable to you.
- Asking "curiosity questions" helps children explore the consequences of their choices.
- Other parenting tools include:
  - o Redirecting children from inappropriate to appropriate behavior.
  - o Deciding what you're going to do and then following through.
  - o Spending quality time with each child.

- In situations of minor conflict between your children, put them all in the same boat.
- Positive time-outs:
  - o Remove children from the conflict.
  - o Allow them to focus on solving the problem.
  - o Are not meant to be a punishment.

- Parents shut down communication with children when they blame, preach, threaten, intimidate, or put the children down.
- When you hold regular family meetings, everyone can help solve problems and set goals, and you build team spirit.
- When problem solving, let every idea be a possibility. No idea is a bad idea. Create an atmosphere of cooperation.
- To teach children about managing money:
  - o Give them an allowance (possibly tied to chores).
  - o Establish budgets for sports, gifts, toys, etc.
  - o Encourage them to save, even small amounts.

WEEK 6 ACTION ITEMS

- Complete the exercises in Week 6.
- Journal about using one of the 12 positive discipline parenting tools or about a challenging event where you wish you had used the parenting tools.
- Have a family meeting using ideas from "How to Conduct Family Meetings" in this chapter.

WEEK 7, DESIGNING A WORKABLE PARENTING PLAN

What You Will Find in Week 7:

• Children's Ages, Needs, and Developmental Stages
• Designing the Parent Plan
• Siblings and the Parent Plan
• Changing the Parent Plan
• Exchanging Information
• Scheduling and Sample Calendars

"Decide together what it is you want to accomplish. Work together respectfully to lay out your parent plan. Work together collaboratively to follow your parent plan."
Carol Delzer, course author

CHILDREN'S AGES, NEEDS, AND DEVELOPMENTAL STAGES

Children's abilities and needs are not the same at four as they are at thirteen. They grow and change. These changes take place in known developmental stages that are fairly predictable, although the exact age these changes occur varies slightly from child to child.

When considering a parenting plan, your children's ages and needs are significant factors. The needs of a young child and the needs of a teenager, for instance, are going to be very different. That may be obvious. Not so obvious are some of the things co-parents can do to help children through these developmental stages.

While you may know your children very well, a solid understanding of the developmental needs of children will make you better able to design an effective parenting plan.

A look at where your children stand developmentally will help you design an age-appropriate plan to meet their needs. Although the information provided here divides recommendations into age groups and developmental norms, parents should remember that each child is an individual.

The Developmental Stages for Children

Separation and divorce are major stressors in a child's life. Designing a parenting plan that considers each child's developmental stage will reduce some of the stress and anxiety at the time of the separation or divorce.

The following information touches just briefly on developmental stages based on the work of developmental psychologist Erik Erikson (1902–1994). For a more in-depth understanding of these stages, I recommend Erikson's work, which includes the study of the roles of nature vs. nurture in a human being's development.

One of Erikson's innovations was the eight stages of psychosocial development that he theorized every person goes through from birth to death. Each stage is based on a conflict of opposites that humans experience, such as trust versus mistrust. A successful resolution (learning how to trust, in our example) results in a favorable outcome developmentally. His primary work on this theory is *Childhood and Society* (1950).

Much of the advice provided below regarding designing parenting plans for different developmental stages came from the Association of Family And Conciliation Courts (AFCC). For more information, go to the Resources section at collaborativecoparenting.com to find a link to AFCC.

It is not necessary to read all of the following stages. For now, just focus on your children's developmental stages and the appropriate parenting plan tips.

The Developmental Stages
Infancy: Birth to 18 Months
Developmental Challenge: Trust vs. Mistrust
Basic Strength: Drive and Hope

During this stage of life, children learn to trust that life is basically okay, and they can have confidence in the future. If children fail to experience trust, they may end up with deep feelings of mistrust and the sense that their needs will never be met.

Infants learn things very quickly. It's natural for them to love, trust, and become attached to their parents when they are held, fed, played with, talked to gently, and their needs are met promptly. Frequent contact with both parents is important, along with predictable routines, affection, and love.

It is important to maintain an infant's routines, particularly the infant's sleep and feeding cycles. Parents should coordinate their schedules to limit disruption to the infant's routine. If one parent is not available to spend a lot of time with the infant, the child will have a very difficult time remembering the absent parent. One objective is for the infant to have meaningful attachments to both parents — and that means time with both.

The transition from infant to toddler takes place gradually. Skill development is rapid in the areas of motor skills (standing, crawling, walking) and communication, from sounds and smiles to simple words. The expression of emotions begins to emerge.

In creating plans for this age group, parents should consider the needs of children this age. The most significant relationship in the first months is generally with the maternal parent, or a significant and constant caregiver. This caretaker role should be supported in the design of a parent plan for an infant up to six months. It is recommended in this period of a child's life that there is a primary/parent caretaker to build basic trust and confidence.

It is critical that the infant-toddler attach to both parents. Gaining this attachment at this stage will give the child the confidence to explore his or her world in the future.

Designing a Parenting Plan for Infants

To develop a healthy attachment to both parents, an infant should not be away from either parent for more than a few days at a time. Extended separation from the primary caregiver should be avoided because infants benefit from having a primary caregiver.

At this age, parenting time with non-residential parents should be several times weekly. This parenting time should provide lots of opportunities for the non-residential parent to nurture the child through activities such as playing, feeding, bathing, soothing, and putting the infant to sleep, whether for a nap or for the night. This will help the non-residential parent maintain or build a close bond with the infant.

If both parents participated in all aspects of childcare on a reasonably consistent basis before the separation, the plan should allow for shared parenting to continue. If the non-primary parent has not previously been involved caring for the infant, parenting the infant for a few hours every few days will help to develop a bond. As this bond forms and grows, the infant will develop the trust needed for extended time with the parent.

As the infant passes the nine-month mark, non-primary parents who have been active caregivers may begin overnights, starting with one a week along with other daytime contact. These overnights should be in familiar surroundings where the infant feels safe.

Communication between the parents about the infant is essential for the infant's easy adjustment to moving between households. The parents should exchange a daily communication log noting eating, sleeping, and diapering patterns, along with any new developments. The daily communication log can be a valuable tool for other developmental stages as well.

Early Childhood: 18 Months to 3 Years
Developmental Challenge: Autonomy vs. Shame
Basic Strengths: Self-control, Courage, and Will

During this stage, toddlers learn to master skills for themselves. Not only do toddlers learn to walk, talk, and feed themselves, they learn finer motor skills as well. Among these is the much-appreciated mastering of toilet training. This is the time for toddlers to build self-esteem as they gain more control over their bodies and acquire new skills, such as the difference between right from wrong. One of the skills during the "Terrible Twos" is the ability to use the powerful word "No!" It may be painful for parents to hear, but expressing will is an important skill in a child's development.

Children also become very vulnerable during this stage. If they are shamed in the process of toilet training or while learning other important skills, they may feel doubt in their own capabilities and suffer low self-esteem as they move toward adulthood.

The period from eighteen months to three years is one of rapid emotional, physical, mental, and social change. Toddlers become more aware of the world around them and form strong attachments to various caregivers, such as parents, grandparents, daycare providers, and close family friends. They become more independent and develop the ability to comfort themselves with a favorite toy or blanket or by sucking their thumb or twirling their hair. Some children may cling to a parent or cry at the separation from one or both parents.

Toddlers also develop the ability to respond to different parenting styles during this time, although they may exhibit some separation anxiety. This resistance to change is normal and does not mean the child will always like one parent over the other. It's just a temporary stage some toddlers go through.

Supporting the child's relationship with the other parent can make exchanges easier. Toddlers seem particularly sensitive to anger and tension between parents, so minimizing negative emotions between you and the other parent is important to the emotional health of your child.

Designing a Parent Plan for Toddlers

Parents with a child of this age should consider:

1. Overnights should be spaced throughout the week, particularly if dealing with an only child.
2. Daily telephone contact (once the child is old enough) at a regular hour may be reassuring to both the children and the absent parent. If nurtured, this is likely something the child will look forward to and appreciate for years.
3. Keeping a picture of the absent parent with the child in the child's room is a good way to support the strong bond you are all working to maintain.
4. Frequent contact between both parents and the child helps everyone establish and maintain stronger relationships.

Play Age: 3 to 5 Years
Developmental Challenge: Initiative vs. Reluctance
Basic Strength: Purpose

During this preschool period, children begin to engage more actively with the outside world. They enjoy other children and begin to copy the adults around them. They make up stories with dolls, toy phones, and miniature cars, experimenting with what they believe people do. They also may initiate play with you and playmates. These preschoolers also start to engage the use of that wonderful word for exploring the world: "Why?"

At this stage, children usually become involved in classic power struggles with their parents. For most children, while they would love to do what they want to do and get their parents to do the same, this is scary because they need to count on their parents for protection, guidance, and nurturing. They also may say what they believe the parent wants to hear, so it's important to remember that what children say in this stage of development does not necessarily reflect their real experience.

Children in preschool years experience a tremendous number of developmental changes and parents need to adjust their parenting styles to accommodate these changes. One of the things that happens is that preschoolers think they are the center of the universe and therefore often feel they are responsible for the divorce.

Children of this age need continued predictability, routine, and structure. Consistent discipline from parent to parent is advisable when possible, and they benefit from blocks of time with each parent. If the child reports parental behavior that causes concern, discuss the matter with the other parent, not the child. In many instances, the child may have misunderstood what happened and talking to the other parent may resolve the issue.

Designing a Parent Plan for Preschoolers

Parents with a child of this age should consider:

1. The amount of childcare each of the parents provided prior to separation

2. The child's temperament

3. The level of conflict between parents

4. The child's familiarity with each parent's home

When both parents have been involved in the child's daily routine, reasonably equal time should be considered. This, of course, depends on how the child is adjusting, ease of transitions between homes, the effectiveness of parental communication, and other factors.

If one parent was minimally involved in the child's daily routine, a few days each week, including a full weekend day, allows the relationship to develop and gives the less involved parent time for his or her care-giving skills to blossom. Additional time and one or two overnights may be added as the child and that parent bond more fully and the child becomes more comfortable moving between two homes.

If one parent is primarily at home with the child, the parenting plan may offer the other parent more weekend time, in addition to some weekday contact.

In situations where both parents are working outside the home at the time of separation and have the child in daycare, parents might consider splitting each weekend in half. That gives the child one full stay-at-home day and overnight with each parent every week, as well as some weekday contact. While this may not be the best solution for the parents, it helps many young children through the early stages of separation.

Some parents find that an every-other-weekend schedule with midweek contact works well. As the child moves through this developmental stage, weekends may be extended to include either Friday or Sunday night or both.

School Age: 6 to 9 Years (Early School Age) and 10 to 12 Years (Preteen)
Developmental Challenge: Industry vs. Inferiority
Basic Strengths: Method and Competence

Early School Age: 6 to 9 years
During this stage, children are capable of learning and creating many new things. As they gain numerous new skills and acquire knowledge, these new capabilities help them develop a sense of industry. Social skills also blossom and begin to develop empathy and a stronger sense of right and wrong. Children who experience unresolved feelings of inferiority among

their peers may develop serious feelings of incompetence and a lack of self-esteem as they grow up.

As the world expands, their most significant relationship is with their schools and neighborhoods. Parents no longer are the complete authorities they once were. Children of this age can usually adjust to different parenting styles more easily than younger children and are more secure with having two residences. This is one of the most flexible stages of development for most children.

This period begins the long, usually more settled, middle years of childhood. Children have greater experience with multiple separations from parents (e.g. school, relatives, friends, sports), but it also is a key time to maximize frequent contact with both parents. This depends on circumstances such as geographical distance, parents' work commitments, the child's activities, temperament and adjustment, and level of conflict between the parents.

Early school-age children understand the concepts of time and routine, so they are more secure than younger children with transitions and the idea of two residences. This flexibility allows parents to be more creative in preparing parenting plans. Use a calendar to inform and remind children of schedules outlined in the parenting plan. If changes can be anticipated and discussed ahead of time, this will ease much of the stress of transitions.

Designing a Parent Plan for Early School Age

1. Plan on one to two overnights a week with the non-residential parent with the understanding that some children still require a home base. Other children do well alternating or splitting weeks.

2. Plan on at least one weekday overnight so that the non-residential parent can fully participate in the child's schooling. Research shows that children with fathers involved in their schooling perform better in school.

3. Another alternative is to plan on alternate weekends with an evening during the week. The weekend could include two or three overnights, depending on the children's needs.

Fun, social activities, and commitments such as piano or soccer practice should be given priority when possible. Children thrive when they adhere to a schedule and need to develop outside interests and friendships during this time. Parents need to support this.

Maintaining consistency in the schedule is important to children. They want to know they are with Mom on certain days and with Dad on the other days. This helps them make plans with friends or know which parent is responsible for getting them to and from their activities.

Pre-teen: 10 to 12 Years

During these pre-teen years, children are preparing to make the leap into puberty and adolescence. Children of this age have a firm understanding of time, future plans, and schedules and are able to balance different values and parental practices that exist in their parents' two residences.

Children of this age also tend to be "rule bound" and may align themselves with one parent during the separation, especially if their parents are at odds with one another and the arguments seem to call on the child to take sides. Children who refuse to see one of the parents might need professional counseling to help them cope with their feelings toward that parent.

Pre-teens should be encouraged to engage in a variety of activities because such involvement helps children develop social and intellectual skills. These skills prepare your children for greater independence later. Children of this age also seem to want more control of their time, so involving them in designing how time is split in the parent plan often is a plus all around and avoids later problems. Pre-teens need to know that their parents will consider their preferences, but as co-parents they will make the ultimate decisions.

Parental support of increased independence contributes to children's self-esteem and confidence.

Designing a Parent Plan for Pre-teens:

1. Pre-teens can do well with many different parenting plans. The most important thing is that they have frequent contact with both parents.

2. Plans should include overnights during the week and on weekends whenever possible.

3. Children should be given the opportunity and privacy to call the other parent.

4. Children's preferences should be considered and respected, but remember that parents still make the final decision.

5. Honoring and accommodating the child's social activities and commitments is important.

Adolescence: 13 to 15 Years (Early Adolescence) and 16 to 18 Years (Late Adolescence)
Developmental Challenge: Identity vs. Role Confusion
Basic Strengths: Devotion and Fidelity

Early Adolescence: 13 to 15 Years

Adolescence is a stage when people are neither children nor adults. Life is getting more complex as they attempt to find their own identity, struggle with social interactions, and grapple with moral issues. Still, young people in this stage still need their family as a base of support and guidance.

Decision-making abilities vary widely among adolescents, as well as from one situation to another. Though they may not show it, young adolescents continue to need the nurturing and oversight of both their parents.

Some adolescents also become competitive with the same sex parent while getting along better with the opposite-sex parent. So girls often have a more difficult time with their mothers and get along better with their fathers, and boys often have a more difficult time with their fathers and get along better with their mothers.

Young people of this age should be encouraged to explore activities and develop social relationships outside the family, but parents will find that these outside interests often compete with the scheduled parenting plan. Adolescents often will prefer to spend time with peers instead of their parents and can become resentful and angry if their wishes are not respected. The challenge for parents is to support their growing independence while maintaining some basic structure and close contact with both parents.

It is appropriate for the adolescents to begin to negotiate their time directly with each parent. It is of paramount importance for parents to talk directly with each other to be certain that the child is safe and accountable.

Designing a Parent Plan for Early Adolescence

Teens' schedules and commitments should be considered in designing the parenting plan, along with the distance between the parents' homes, each parent's work schedule or other obligations, the adolescent's temperament and wishes, and recognition of a young person's need for unstructured time.

Although many different plans may work for adolescents, some options include:

1. Alternating seven-day periods, with or without mid-week time

2. Alternating long weekends, with or without mid-week time

3. Providing a home base with some time with the non-residential parent during the week and on weekends

During this developmental period, adolescents may articulate a desire for a home base because of the growing importance of their own network, friends, school life, and outside activities. Both parents can increase contact by making themselves available to drive teens to activities and by attending athletic, academic, or other events. This allows for maximum parental involvement in activities important in the adolescent's life.

Late Adolescence: 16 to 18 years

Parents of sixteen- to eighteen-year-olds should encourage and support their older children by helping them through:

1. The gradual and healthy separation from both parents.

2. The development of an individual identity.

3. The establishing of a sense of self with regard to rules and regulations of society, school, and peer groups.

4. An understanding of sexual and other feelings in the context of relationships.

Designing a Parent Plan for Late Adolescence: 16 to 18 years

Older adolescents do well with many different plan models. Communication between parents is key, especially regarding driving, dating, curfews, and overnights away from both homes.

Adolescents are particularly vulnerable to changes within the family and to pressure from outside the family. Maintaining stability and consistency can be challenging because adolescents' feelings about the world around them are often variable and intense.

Increased schoolwork, extracurricular activities, jobs, friendships, romantic relationships, and sports are often more important than time with family or either parent. They are looking toward their future and might feel annoyed, resentful, or panicked that the separation or divorce changed the world as they knew it.

While adolescents appear to be ready for increased independence, there remains a need for consistency, support, rules, and meaningful time with both parents. Parents should be aware of an adolescent's need to be consulted, informed, and involved when making plans. It's best to remain flexible when possible while maintaining age-appropriate controls.

Siblings

Another factor to consider when thinking through your parenting plan is its effect on siblings. Do you spend individual time with each child or move siblings back and forth from home to home together?

Keep in mind that the sibling relationship generally becomes stronger due to the divorce. In many cases, siblings come to see themselves as the one constant in this time of turmoil and change in the relationship between their parents. An older sibling may take on a protective role or help a younger sibling transition between homes more easily. A younger sibling may feel comfort in being able to look up to an older sibling for reassurance. A divorce can often result in a closer sibling relationship, so many times, especially in the first months of separation or divorce, it's wise to keep the siblings together.

Designing a parent plan that honors the sibling relationship as well as the different ages of your children is important. If the children are close in age—say, within two or three years of one another—the parent plan (absent any special needs) should keep the children together most of the time. If the sibling age gap is wide, their developmental needs and interests may warrant a parent plan where the children are on different schedules. Even then, it is important for them to spend some time together at both Mom's house and Dad's house.

Interestingly, the quality of the relationship between siblings is often directly linked to the quality of the relationship parents have with each child individually. Strengthening your relationship with each child will help your children grow closer.

A Change in Plans

When we first divorced, my daughter's father and I agreed upon a parenting plan that remained consistent and worked well from the time Jessica was three years old until she was six years old.

When Jessica was six, however, she asked me if she could join the local soccer team with her best friend. What immediately concerned me was that the soccer schedule of practices and games conflicted with our parent plan. We'd developed such a respectful and workable routine, I did not want to do anything to change our collaborative relationship.

In my family law practice, I have seen parents want to change their current parent plan for good reason only to end up in conflict. Yet I knew that due to a child's developmental needs, parent plans do need to change.

After several months of Jessica's persistence, I decided to discuss the idea with Jessica's father. I was surprised at how easy the conversation was and how well it all ended. I explained that Jessica had been showing an interest in playing soccer, but I was concerned about how it would interfere with his parenting time. We ended up having a great discussion about the value of team sports, especially because Jessica was an only child. Both of us agreed to adjust the parenting plan to make her involvement possible.

Jessica's soccer turned out to be one of the highlights of her development and a joy to both of us as parents. It was a healthy physical and emotional outlet for her and I delighted in the experience of being a soccer mom while her father became her biggest fan and cheerleader at the games.

Jessica played soccer throughout her school years, including playing on competitive teams. Something I had feared might create conflict in our parent plan was a positive experience all around.

Designing Workable Parent Agreements

A well-written parent agreement will be helpful to your co-parent relationship. It is an important document and deserves enough time to consider all possibilities.

Start by understanding that the parent plan is your agreement. This means that you may add whatever information is needed to support the two of you in your working relationship.

Most parent plans and court-ordered custody agreements are written by someone other than the parents. These agreements often contain information the parents did not decide on or agree to. Instead, the information likely was placed in the parent plan by a well-meaning mediator or attorney who believes he or she knows what works for most parents. This does not mean the same information works for you.

It's your agreement and I recommend that you take charge. The courts have no prohibition against parents adding provisions to their parenting plans. In fact, the court has minimal requirements about what is mandatory in a parent agreement.

What is required in the parent agreement is set by state and county court rules, so before preparing yours, check to determine what the minimum requirements are in your area. This is the part a mediator or attorney *can* help you with.

Generally, the courts require a determination of Legal Custody and Physical Custody. Let's look at what those terms mean:

> *Legal custody* *is the decision-making process about the children's health, education, and welfare. Courts encourage parents to have joint legal custody and share in the decision-making process.*

> *Physical custody* *is where the children are going to live. The courts require that the parents select "joint" or "sole" physical custody. Joint physical custody does not necessarily mean equal or 50/50 parenting time. It does mean that both parents have a substantial amount of time with the child.*

If one parent has sole physical custody, the other parent will usually have parenting time outlined in the specified agreement.

If one parent is unable to cooperate or unfit to make decisions regarding the children, the court will award sole legal custody to the parent who is capable.

The best parent plans establish consistency for the children in what can be a very inconsistent time.

The information here is intended to help parents understand they have many options to select from. If you already have an agreement or a court-ordered parent plan, this information can be used in the future when you modify or expand your existing agreement.

You can make an addendum or an amendment to your existing parent plan by adding some of the options or by replacing an existing section of your agreement. This should always be done in writing and signed by both parents. It can be one page long or twenty pages long, but should detail how you agree to raise your children together.

Ideas For Parent Plans

- Declaration or mission statement
- Name and date of birth of each child
- Standards of conduct for parents
- Parent responsibilities, decisions, and appointments
- Parents' access to information and records
- School and education
- Child care and nanny
- Time spent with each parent, including school, summer holidays
- Transportation to/from each home
- How to modify the parent plan
- Provisions for catastrophic events
- Religious affiliation and training
- Grandparents' visitation

I have seen and designed thousands of parenting plans. Some parenting plans have been very lengthy and specific, and others have been brief and non-specific. Among the non-standard things I've seen people include in the parenting plan are specifics such as "no fast food on school days," "no exposure to second-hand smoke," or the stipulation that neither parent use alcohol or drugs during their parenting time or twenty-four hours before their time with the children begins. Parents also sometimes agree on issues such as rules regarding motorcycles or the introduction of significant others in the parenting plan.

Many challenges arise in the course of co-parenting, so it's good to have a plan in place that outlines how to handle these issues in advance. This avoids conflict in the future. For instance, how much advance notice does each of you need to give the other in choosing vacation time? Who is in charge of scheduling routine medical and dental appointments?

When parents are communicating well, they can create flexible agreements with less specific detail. When parents are challenged by communication, a more specific agreement that outlines the details of their co-parent relationship helps reduce the risk of conflict.

My daughter's father and I created a detailed parenting agreement that was filed in the court with our marriage settlement agreement. Within a year of signing our agreement, we began sharing our daughter's time based on an oral agreement that was different from the written agreement filed in court. It worked for us because we had good communication and cooperated with one another and did not need to have the specific details in writing. This would not work for parents still experiencing conflict.

How Do I Get Started?

You may want to start out with a mission statement like the one you designed in Week 2. As a reminder, a mission statement helps keep both of you focused on your goal.

So yours might read something like this:

As we design our parent plan, we will act together as co-parents in the best interest of our child.

Sharing Time

How you share your children's time will vary based on their ages and temperaments, the distance between houses, work schedules, and numerous other factors.

Determine in a calendar month when the children will be at Mom's house and when the children will be at Dad's house.

CO-PARENT MONTHLY CALENDAR

☐ Parent A:_____

☐ Parent B:_____

Mon.	Tues.	Wed.	Thurs.	Fri.	Sat.	Sun.

notes: _____
_____
_____
_____
_____

HOLIDAY SCHEDULE

Write "Parent 1" or "Parent 2" (or "Mom" and "Dad") in each space. Just fill in the holidays that are important to you.

Holiday	Every Year Parent 1 / Parent 2	Even Years Parent 1 / Parent 2	Odd Years Parent 1 / Parent 2
New Year's Day			
Martin Luther King Day			
Lincoln's Birthday			
President's Day weekend			
Spring Break			
Mother's Day			
Memorial Day weekend			
Father's Day			
Summer Break, 1st half			
Summer Break, 2nd half			
July 4th			
Labor Day weekend			
Columbus Day weekend			
Halloween			
Veteran's Day weekend			
Thanksgiving Day			
Thanksgiving weekend			
Winter Break, 1st half			
Winter Break, 2nd half			
Christmas			
Christmas Eve			
Hanukah			
New Year's Eve			
New Year's Day			
Child's birthday			

Mother's birthday			
Father's birthday			
Year-round school breaks			
Other holidays:			

Information Exchange and Access

Here some other things you might include in your parent plan:

- Contact Information: Both parents shall give addresses and phone numbers to one another, the school, and all child-care providers.
- Records: Both parents shall have access to all medical and school records. It is our intent that both parents know about the children's medical and educational needs. Both parents agree to coordinate efforts regarding transportation, school conferences, and consultations.
- Phone Access: Both parents agree that the children shall have reasonable phone access to both parents and that both have reasonable phone access to the children.

Communication

Both parents shall regularly discuss the children's needs and progress. As parents, we agree to inform the other of significant events during the time the children are with us and to do so before, or at the time, the children change residences. This includes information about school, activities, events, and medication as well as the children's feelings, moods, and physical health. Maintaining a daily log that travels with the children can help keep both parents informed.

Decisions about the Children

1. Appointments and Decisions: Neither parent shall make any arrangement or commitment that involves their co-parent's time or effort without first obtaining agreement from their co-parent. The only exception is reserving a spot in an activity pending their co-parent's approval.

2. Daily Decisions: The parent who has the children shall make the small day-to-day decisions as needed during his or her parent time.

3. Emergency Decisions: Emergency medical care necessary for the preservation of the children, or to prevent a further serious condition, may be authorized without consulting the co-parent, but the co-parent is to be notified as soon as possible. Parents shall make every effort to immediately contact their co-parent in the event of a medical emergency. Each parent shall notify the other within two hours of any illness or accident requiring medical attention or any medical emergency involving the children and within two hours of any life-threatening illness or accident.

4. Medical Decisions: Decisions about the children's medical care shall be made jointly.

5. Dental/Orthodontia Decisions: Decisions about the children's dental care shall be made jointly.

6. Counseling Decisions: Decisions about the children's counseling needs shall be made jointly.

7. Out-of-State Travel: Both parents agree that they will not take the minor children out of the state without a prior written agreement from their co-parent or a court order.

8. First Right of Refusal: In the event that either parent is absent from the minor children during their parenting time for more than eight hours, that parent shall provide the other parent with first right of refusal to care for the minor children.

9. Grandparent Rights: Both parents agree that the maternal and paternal grandparents shall have reasonable rights of visitation with the minor children.

Conduct

1. Respect: Neither parent shall do anything that would estrange the children from the other parent or impair the children's love and respect for the other parent.

2. Activities: Both parents are free to attend the children's activities, even if the children are not residing with that parent at the time. The non-resident parent shall not interfere in the children's schedule or with the resident parent's agreements during each scheduled time.

3. Consistent Contact: Consistent, routine contact with both parents is an important goal of the parent plan.

School and Education

Both parents recognize the significance of education and will strive to provide the children with a quality educational experience, including, but not limited to, the following:

1. Conferences: Both parents may attend school conferences, open houses, and progress reviews.

2. Report Cards: Both parents will share report cards and progress reports with their co-parent.

3. School Decisions: Decisions about the children's school, grades, and any special program placement will be made jointly.

4. School Expenses—Mandatory: Parents shall share equally the mandatory school expenses.

5. School Expenses—Non-mandatory: Parents shall share equally the non-mandatory school expenses based on (choose one: oral or written) mutual agreement.

6. Homework: Both parents will help with homework and provide the time and space for homework to be completed during their parenting time.

~ EXERCISES ~

Your Parent Plan

Take time to consider what new ideas or points you would like to propose to your co-parent to include in your co-parent plan.

_____

_____

_____

_____

_____

_____

Given the information you read in the developmental section, what are some of the age-specific considerations you and your co-parent need to take into account in the details of your parent plan?

_____

_____

_____

_____

_____

_____

REVIEW OF WEEK 7

- Divorce can be stressful for all children, and they have different needs at different ages.
- Siblings often grow closer as a result of divorce.
- Even if an attorney or a mediator originally wrote your parenting plan, you and your co-parent can agree to change it.
- Parenting plans detail how you will raise your children, including areas such as parent responsibilities, education, child care, religion, and time spent with each parent.
- When deciding how to divide your children's time, determine what will work best for your children, yourself, and your co-parent.
- When co-parents have trouble communicating, a very detailed parenting plan can help reduce the risk of conflict.
- Not everyone needs a detailed parenting plan in writing that must be followed at all times.
- Small, day-to-day decisions should be made by the parent who has the children.
- It's a good idea to fill out a schedule in advance showing where your children will spend each holiday.
- A parenting plan can include very detailed guidelines, such as:
  - o Both parents will share report cards and progress reports with their co-parent.
  - o Both parents are free to attend the children's activities.
  - o Decisions about the children's dental care will be made jointly.

WEEK 7 ACTION ITEMS

- Complete the exercises in Week 7.
- Review the developmental stage of your children. Journal about a time when you were this age.
- Review your Mission Statement that you wrote in Week 2 and journal about your efforts to implement it.

WEEK 8, SPECIAL CHALLENGES

What You Will Find in Week 8:

- Long-Distance Parenting
- Parallel Parenting
- Impacts of Secondhand Smoke
- Information about Drugs and Alcohol
- Information about Addiction
- Information about Domestic Violence
- Significant Others

Some divorces and breakups face more challenges than others. Sometimes these challenges were visible in the family before the breakup, and sometimes they appeared during the process of divorce. Special challenges may include one or more of the following:

- Long-distance parenting
- Parallel parenting (when parents cannot communicate)
- Children's exposure to secondhand smoke

- Alcohol and drug abuse by one or both parents
- Domestic violence
- Significant others

Many of these issues are the topics of entire books, so it's difficult to go into the depth needed to thoroughly address them here. I encourage you to seek help to deal with any challenges that are beyond the scope of this program. For names and links to specific support groups and other information, check out the Resources section on our website, collaborativecoparenting.com.

LONG-DISTANCE PARENTING

Changing residences is a part of every divorce, even if only one parent moves out of the area. The average American family moves to a new home every five years. As separate lives take shape for divorcing parents, sometimes one of the parents decides to move away for a new job or to gain the support of extended family. This move can create some challenges that will disrupt the parent's contact with the children.

It is in the best interests of your children to have continuous and frequent contact with both parents, regardless of where the parents live. Children need both parents. So what happens if one moves away? How do you keep the relationship vital between the children and a parent now living several towns — or even states — away?

This situation requires extra work for the co-parents, but long-distance parenting or a move away from the area can be managed with cooperation. The goal is that the relationship between the children and parents continue to grow and thrive. When parents are unable to work together cooperatively, a long-distance parental relationship is not advised.

Keeping a long-distance relationship with your children alive and well requires the assistance and positive attitude of both parents. The parent who becomes the primary caretaker and lives with the children most of the time can be instrumental in the success or failure of the long-distance parent relationship. The long-distance parent needs to be willing to travel to see the children as often as possible and not always expect the children to do all the traveling.

> **Long-distance parenting agreements may include any of the following:**
>
> - *How parents share the children's time.*
> - *How parents divide the holiday and school vacations.*
> - *What mode of transportation will be used as the child travels back and forth between homes.*
> - *Who makes reservations and arrangements for travel and who bears the costs.*
> - *How co-parents will exchange information about the children from a distance.*
> - *How the long-distance parent and child will keep in touch.*

I once had a client whose ex-wife remarried and moved six hundred miles away with the former couple's six-year-old son. The boy was too young to fly alone from one town to another, so, for a year, Dad flew to the new city once a month to pick him up and bring him back to the father's town for a three-day weekend. Mom flew up to retrieve the boy.

It was a stretch financially, but the trips prepared the boy to fly back and forth alone once he matured and was able to do so legally. I was proud of my client, the father, for his resolve to maintain close contact with his son, whom he adored, and of the mother for her contribution to making the arrangement work.

161

Ideally, these long-distance arrangements include a written agreement between the parents that outlines how they work. This will avoid misunderstandings and conflict later on.

Technological Tools

Technological tools can ease the distance and help maintain strong ties between the children and the long-distance parent. These tools are great ways for all families to keep in touch, even if your two residences are right across town.

- Obtain a home phone or cell phone plan with unlimited long distance both for the children and parents.
- Scan homework, essays, projects, and teacher feedback and send it to the long-distant parent.
- Use IM (instant messaging) to stay in touch. Many companies now allow unlimited texting on plans, some for a nominal cost each month.
- Videotape activities and important moments for the parent who misses these occasions because of distance.
- Obtain cell phones with photo-sending capabilities for the children and the long-distance parent.
- Install cameras on computers to allow "video-chatting" or webcam communication between the children and the long-distance parent.
- Create a family website or blog where anyone in the family can post photos, notes on trips or outings, or anything they want everyone in the family to know. This can generally be obtained for free.

Remember, above all, you are still a family!

Making Long-distance Parenting Work

The long-distance parent can ease the situation for the children when they visit. Some ideas include:

- Picking colors or themes over the phone for the children's areas and then working on the project together when the children arrive
- Creating a Lego city that's always growing
- Building a tree house together over time
- Having traditions they engage in whenever the children visit the long-distance parent's city. Maybe the parent and children volunteer somewhere together or always go to the same diner. Maybe they both are slowly discovering all of the bike trails in the city. All it has to be is something they do together that makes the children feel that this is their town too.
- The long-distance parent can visit the children in their hometown sometimes. They can arrange to stay in a nearby hotel or, if possible, in the children's primary residence.

Parents who help retain the parent-child bond give a special gift to their children. Imagine how much your children will appreciate this in the future. Teaching children to bond will reap benefits years from now.

Just remember, the adult decision to relocate does not change the fact that children have a right to have meaningful relationships with both parents. With commitment and creativity, both parents can work together to honor that right.

The Obstacle in Our Path

In ancient times, a king had a boulder placed on a roadway. Then he hid himself and watched to see if anyone would remove the huge rock. Some of the king's wealthiest merchants and courtiers came by and simply walked around it. Many loudly blamed the king for not keeping the roads clear, but none did anything about getting the stone out of the way.

Then a peasant came along carrying a load of vegetables. Upon approaching the boulder, the peasant laid down his burden and tried to move the stone to the side of the road. After much pushing and straining, he finally succeeded.

After the peasant picked up his load of vegetables, he noticed a purse in the road where the boulder had been. The purse contained many gold coins and a note from the king indicating that the gold was for the person who removed the boulder from the roadway.

The peasant learned what many of us never understand. Every obstacle presents an opportunity to improve our condition.

Parallel Parenting
When Parents Cannot Communicate

As you've learned, collaborative co-parenting is possible when you work toward keeping the conflict low and parents do a good job in communicating with each other about their children. But what do you do when you cannot communicate with your children's other parent or the other parent is not capable of getting along with you on any level? "Parallel parenting" is for parents who are unable to work together.

What is Parallel Parenting?

Parallel parenting takes its name from the early development stage when children do not have the ability to play with one another. Researchers have noted that up until about three years of age, toddlers do not know how to share while playing. They may play side by side (or parallel to one another, each in their own world) while generally ignoring one another, but they are not playing cooperatively. They do not yet have the skills to interact. About age three, children move from parallel play to cooperative play.

Parallel parenting is the process of parenting with very little contact between the parents because you are not capable of parenting together *yet*. Parents who've learned to parent together are engaging in collaborative co-parenting.

Definition:

In collaborative co-parenting, you work together in the best interests of the children.

In parallel parenting, you work separately in the best interests of the children.

The backbone of parallel parenting usually includes a very specific written parenting plan or court-ordered custody plan that must be followed exactly by both parents. When court-appointed mediators work with parents to design a parent plan, they determine how much detail needs to be included. When the court mediator sees parents with a high level of conflict and little or no ability to communicate, the court recommendations are written very specifically. These court-ordered recommendations go into the detail of describing not only the specific time and day of how the parents will share the children's time, but also how and where they will start and end their parenting time, how they will exchange information, and how certain things that have been problems in the past will now be handled.

These "behavior requests" are things parents can and cannot do while parenting the children. For instance, it might have to be put into writing that the parents cannot make negative remarks about the other parent in front of the children, or that the parents cannot argue when the children are around. Or maybe the recommendation says a parent who has failed to pick the children up, leaving everyone waiting, must call if he or she is going to be more than fifteen minutes late.

For parents, the first step is disengagement from the other parent. When a pattern of conflict has persisted between parents for some time, the ability to disengage from the conflict can be challenging. Disengaging gives parents the chance to learn new ways to communicate with minimal emotional engagement.

This box has some tips for disengaging from the triggers of dysfunctional patterns of communication when you and your co-parent are parallel parenting.

Parallel parenting assumes that both parents have parenting skills, although those styles or the circumstances have put them in conflict. In cases where there is mental illness, abuse, serious substance addictions, or a complete lack of parenting skills, parallel parenting is not appropriate.

Marilyn and Collin

Marilyn and Collin were pillars of the church, where Collin was an associate pastor in a large evangelical congregation. They were pillars, that is, until the church was rocked by divorce—theirs.

After fifteen years of marriage and twelve years as pastor, Collin was discovered having an affair with a parishioner. Marilyn was more shocked then anyone and quickly filed for divorce.

Marilyn had lost all trust in Collin, and, consequently, couldn't stand to be in the same room with him. This made mediation, including working out a parenting plan, difficult. Because of these challenges, the mediator suggested they parallel parent, at least until the rawness of the situation lessened.

Collin and Marilyn have been divorced five years now and Marilyn can now co-parent more cooperatively. She still keeps communication with Collin to a minimum, mostly using e-mail, but they are able to talk about important matters concerning their children.

Communication Tips in Parallel Parenting Arrangements

- *Have a specific parenting plan in place that both parents can follow. This avoids having anything to "hash out."*
- *Do not get into debates about parenting plans or parenting styles. Instead, follow the written agreement.*
- *When communication is necessary, do it by e-mail. Putting your thoughts in writing gives you time to measure your words and make sure the tone is not argumentative.*
- *Do not bicker over things that led to conflict in the past.*
- *Do not communicate about small issues regarding your child. Pick your battles carefully, always focusing on the most important issues.*
- *Avoid arguing when the other parent makes statements that could pull you into conflict.*
- *When your children are with you, don't criticize the other parent.*
- *Do not tell the other parent how to parent or take it personally when the other parent tells you how to parent.*
- *Keep an open mind that as time passes communication skills will increase, and you can replace parallel parenting with a collaborative parenting partnership.*
- *Use a neutral third party to share important information when necessary.*

Exposure to Secondhand Smoke

If you are a smoker, eliminating smoking is hard because of the addictive nature of smoking. But who comes first, you or your children? Or try putting it this way: Who comes first, your children or smoking?

Both the U.S. Environmental Protection Agency and the Centers for Disease Control have determined that the health of infants and young children can be severely harmed by secondhand smoke. Infants and children are especially vulnerable to the poisons found in secondhand smoke because their bodies are so small and organs such as the lungs are still developing.

Exposure to secondhand smoke usually happens in the home or car and can cause the following ill effects in infants and children:

- Frequent serious respiratory conditions such as bronchitis and pneumonia
- Increased and worsening asthma attacks
- Acute middle ear infections
- Weaker lungs, which increases the chance of other health problems
- A greater risk of dying from Sudden Infant Death Syndrome (SIDS) for babies
- Increased respiratory symptoms such as coughing, wheezing, and breathlessness in school-age children
- Long-term poor health

Where Can I Smoke?

Children cannot protect themselves from the dangers of secondhand smoke if the adults around them insist on smoking. There is no safe level of secondhand smoke, according to the Surgeon General, the nation's leading spokesperson on matters of public health. The only way to fully protect your children is eliminating smoking in all indoor spaces, including the car.

Secondhand smoke permeates the house and car, lingering after the cigarette is put out, so there is no safe time or place to smoke in enclosed areas that are part of your children's world.

Here are a few more things you can do to protect your children from secondhand smoke:

• Make sure daycare centers and schools are smoke free.
• Insist that no one smoke around your children.
• Smoking by a window or next to a fan is not enough.
• If you smoke, quit for your children's sake. One place to find help is the Resources section of collaborativeparenting. com.

Drugs and Alcohol

If you or your children's other parent abuse drugs or alcohol, it is critical to your children's well-being that the person abusing these substances makes a commitment to change. Change involves learning new habits, along with finding new ways of facing the world and making decisions.

It might help to start off by remembering that everyone makes mistakes. The true measure of recovery is whether you learn more about yourself and grow from your mistakes or whether you blame others and make excuses for your shortcomings. Once you begin to learn, change, and grow, you are on the road to recovery.

What is Drug and Alcohol Abuse?

Let's look at the elements of addiction:

Elements of Addiction

- The user has no control over using or not
- Continued use despite adverse consequences
- An addict is a person who uses even though he or she knows it is causing problems.
- Craving the drug or alcohol
- The user is preoccupied with getting and using the drug or alcohol
- Denial

The intense craving temporarily blinds the user to the risks and consequences of using or the fact they have a problem. Sometimes the user is the last one to admit or know they have a problem.

Addiction gets in the way of being the best parent possible because it often overtakes all else, including our basic good parenting instincts.

The next page outlines some parenting traits of both addicted parents and parents who truly have their children's best interests at heart.

Ideal Parenting Traits	Addicted Parent Traits
Basic Factors: • Food and clothing are provided for the children.	Basic Factors: • Feeding the addiction sometimes comes before providing food and clothing for the children.
Parents encourage development • Parents promote school success and attendance is regular. • Play activities for the children are available. • Parents eat, read, and play with the children. • Parents teach value of structured day, such as meal times, bed times, etc.	Parents neglect development • Addicted parents may let schoolwork and school attendance slide. • Addicted parents may fail to keep the children occupied in play or "forget" to take the children to activities the children once attended. • Addicted parents spend less time or very little time eating with, reading to, or playing with the children. • Structure may go out the door. Meal times and bed times are no longer observed.
Nurturing	Nurturing
• Parent is physically and emotionally responsive to the children through hugging, cuddling, expressions of love, and a consistent manner of responding. • Discipline is not harsh, is consistent, and is age-appropriate. • Parent promotes resilience and problem-solving skills. • Parent avoids frequent moves to create a feeling of physical stability.	• Parent no longer is physically and emotionally responsive to the children through hugging, cuddling, expressions of love, and a consistent manner of responding. • Discipline often is harsh, inconsistent, and fails to be age-appropriate. • Parent fails to model how to solve problems. • Parent may move frequently, making it difficult for the children to establish friends, do well in school, and be part of a familiar community.
Environmental Safety	Environmental Safety
• Parent provides safe living space and supervision. • Parent teaches safety practices and enforces safe habits such as using seatbelts in cars, precautions regarding strangers, and other age-appropriate behaviors. • Access to social networks and family support is valued and nurtured.	• Living space may not be safe and the parent may fail to supervise the children. • Parent often fails to teach the children basic safety measures. • Access to social network and family support falls apart as the addiction takes over the substance-abusing parent's life.

These lists should help you determine if your children may be at risk because of drug or alcohol abuse. If these issues are putting your children in danger, this matter belongs in your local family court. For further information about groups that can help alcoholics and drug addicts, go to the Resources section at collaborativeparenting.com.

Justin and Carmen

Eighteen months after they began dating, Justin and Carmen had a child, a son named Troy. During this time, Justin drank almost daily. He was a happy drinker, but as jobs came and went, Carmen came to see his dependence on alcohol as a huge problem.

His drinking soon became the subject of many arguments and Carmen decided she didn't want to be with Justin anymore — even though he was an attentive father to Troy. Carmen and little Troy moved into an apartment about an hour away from the home they had shared with Justin.

For the next six years, Carmen put great effort into keeping the relationship between Troy and his father going. She called Justin every few weeks to arrange a father-son visit and Justin was always happy to have Troy come for the weekend. He never initiated these visits himself, but Carmen was OK with that. In fact, setting the schedule was a bonus to Carmen. That way these visits fit more conveniently into her life.

This arrangement worked smoothly until the day Troy, then seven, came home with stories of the all-night poker party he had attended at his dad's house. A man had tried to get him to smoke a cigar and "pretty girls" were there. When Carmen questioned Justin about Troy's story, Justin's response was, "So what? He had fun."

That was it for Carmen. She now questioned how she ever trusted "flakey, alcohol-impaired" Justin to know how to care for a young boy. Carmen never called Justin to arrange visits again—and Justin never called Carmen. From the night of the poker party until Troy was in his twenties, Troy never saw his father again.

Now, years later, Carmen feels badly that she didn't work harder to keep Justin's drinking and other circumstances from ending the visits between Troy and his father. Troy, thirty, has trouble bonding in relationships—an issue Carmen worries is due to the sudden severing of the father-son relationship when Troy was young.

Balancing the important need for every child to have two parents with issues of safety can be a challenge. It is my perspective and the perspective of child development specialists that parents need to do whatever is possible to allow children to know both parents. Sometimes this means supervised visits with the children for the parent whose judgment is not child-focused.

Whatever it takes, children need both of their parents.

How Addictions Affect Children

One question that arises is how parental addictions affect children. Some children survive these unfavorable experiences and develop strong convictions that they will never fall into the addictive behavior of their parent—and they don't.

Other children suffer fallout from the experience, including struggling with addictive behavior as adults themselves. Chemically dependent homes expose children to more disappointment, neglect, loneliness, anger, and abuse. In addition, children exposed to addicted parents are known to be at significantly greater risk of the following problems:

• Emotional problems, such as depression or anxiety
• Physical health problems
• Learning problems, including difficulty with cognitive and verbal skills and abstract thinking. This group of children also has more learning disabilities, repeats grades more often, and has higher rates of truancy, delinquency, dropping out, and expulsion.

As you can see, parents with addiction issues need to get their lives in order immediately for the sake of their children. Getting help for your addiction now will improve your children's emotional and physical health, educational achievement, and home life.

You also can help your children by being a better parent once you are in recovery. Teaching your children that people make mistakes and that it's possible to move on from those mistakes will give them a hopeful attitude about the future.

> ### Common Beliefs in Families Experiencing Addiction
>
> • *Do as I say, not as I do.*
> • *Don't talk about problems.*
> • *It's not OK to express feelings openly.*
> • *Never talk about what goes on at home to other people.*
> • *Don't rock the boat.*
> • *Don't talk, don't trust, don't feel.*

And while it's important to protect children from exposure to addiction, this must also be balanced with a child's need to know both parents.

174

Violence

If domestic violence was an ongoing issue in your relation-ship, it can have a great impact on the divorce process. Clients should advise their attorney or court mediator if they are in danger or if there has been a history of domestic violence.

These professionals will ask you questions about the nature of the abuse. It is common, for instance, for divorcing spouses to report domestic violence occurring only in the breakup pro-cess when stress and harmful emotions are at their highest. In fact, many instances of domestic violence occur after a couple has separated.

If a history of violence in the relationship exists, this will have a negative effect on the children. Parents who are per-petrators or victims of violence should seek counseling and appropriate intervention programs. Domestic violence should never happen to anyone, but it does. The first thing to know is there is help available.

Types of Domestic Violence

There are many types of domestic violence including push-ing, shoving, physical intimidation, verbal threats, hitting, and economic isolation. Some of the categories of domestic violence include:

- **Physical**: Physical force against the other partner where one person kicks, hits, shoves, towers over, throws things at, or burns the other partner.
- **Sexual**: Forcing a partner to take part in a sexual act without consent.
- **Emotional**: Threats, destruction of a partner's property, threats against pets or loved ones, stalking, intimidating be-havior, or restricting the freedom of a partner.

- **Situational**: Violence that occurs at the end of a relationship that did not occur before or was extremely rare prior to the breakup.

How Domestic Violence Affects Children

Children exposed to domestic violence have a higher risk of:

- Emotional problems, such as anxiety and depression
- Engaging in conflict and violence themselves
- Antisocial behavior
- Problems at school, including fighting and expulsion
- Challenges with future relationships

Having a Safety Plan

Most experts on domestic violence strongly recommend that people facing domestic violence issues have a safety plan. Communicate with an advocate or domestic violence hotline for advice in advance. They can help you formulate a plan. Here are some tips for putting together your plan:

- Consult with a family law attorney.
- Obtain a restraining order through your local family court.
- Know the route to police and fire stations and hospitals.
- Know what nearby public places have twenty-four-hour access.
- If you leave by car, lock the doors immediately. Have a hidden set of car keys in case your attacker steals your keys.
- Think of a safe place close to home where a friend could pick you up in case you can't get to your car or don't have one.

- Plan a code word or phrase to use on the telephone so your friend knows you need help. Pick a code word that means that person should call 911 for you.
- If you feel comfortable, tell your neighbors so they will call the police if something suspicious is happening in your home.
- Keep copies of important documents in a safe place.

New Significant Others

Single parents need social lives too, yet the logistics of dating are tricky. How do you nurture a new relationship in a week already filled with work, homework, and spending quality time with your children? What happens when your children signal they are opposed to your dating or don't like the idea of a new person becoming a part of your lives? Children can become very possessive of their parents, especially at the time of divorce.

When the person feeling insecure is you, remember that it's normal for a former spouse's new significant other to arouse insecurities, jealousy, competition, or doubt. Try to keep in mind that insecurities are normal feelings. How we handle those feelings is what's important.

I recommend that parents date their new significant other when the children are not around—ideally when

Handling Feelings of Insecurity

- *View these feelings as thoughts, not something to act on.*
- *Have a dialogue with your feelings, like you learned in "Managing Emotions," Week 4.*
- *Refer to your co-parenting mission statement and its priorities.*
- *Focus on the children's best interests.*
- *Remember this is a business partnership.*

they are at the other parent's home. Do not rush to introduce a new significant other to your children and wait before inviting the new significant other to do activities with you and your children. Inviting a new significant other into your family too soon can be disastrous for everyone, including you. Remember that your children need you. A new significant other can feel threatening to their time and relationship with you.

Once the time is right, getting used to changes in relationships takes time for everyone involved and does not happen instantly. The web of how the new significant other fits in does not add just one additional dynamic, but several. The new significant other (say, the dad's new girlfriend) does not just have a relationship with Dad, but conceivably with the children, with Dad's friends who were Mom's friends, and with Dad's extended family, who were once Mom's in-laws.

This new web of relationships sometimes makes blending families together more challenging than creating the original family. Each time we add a new person to the mix, the web of personalities expands.

But with creativity, maturity, patience, and a focus on the children, the addition of the new personalities can be a positive mix if you can come to view new significant others as part of a potentially larger web of supportive, encouraging adults in your children's lives. One great (and amazing!) example of this is the Nirvana Mommas.

> *Wait to Introduce a New Significant*
> *Other to Your Children*
> *Until the Divorce is Over and Final.*

The Nirvana Mommas

I recently had an inspiring day when I met the Nirvana Mommas, Jill and Shelley. One is the ex-wife and the other is the new wife of the same man. These two women broke the stereotype and decided to become friends while supporting one another in raising their sons. To Shelley's son, Connor, Jill is the "other momma." As they put it: "We created a relationship where, together, we make choices to ensure our children are as unaffected by divorce as humanly possible... Together we co-parent two little boys who see us through a child's unaffected prism of innocence and love."

Their story helped me believe anything is possible in a co-parenting relationship. Here is their story:

"We never thought we'd end up divorced young moms. *Ever.* But it happened. Then our lives collided when Jill married Shelley's ex-husband. Though the collision of the new-wife and ex-wife's lives is hardly uncommon, our reaction to it was. We refused to perpetuate the negative, broken family stereotype. In doing so, we've preserved our sanity and ensured that our children are as unaffected by divorce as humanly possible.

"Young, divorced moms have a lot in common. Even the new wife and ex-wife have a lot in common (yes, in addition to their taste in men!). We just wish they'd realize it. When the collision of their lives becomes inevitable, they're both in for one hell of a ride. It's certain both women's perfect pictures evaporated somewhere along the way. Both of them had long-held expectations of life that suddenly ended up in a tangled mess like a heap of dirty laundry on the bathroom floor.

"We realized that we had a lot in common as young, divorced moms finding our way in life. We were on similar journeys. By simply recognizing and embracing this fact, we became great friends while putting our children first. Though they don't happen overnight, relationships like ours are attainable. It's not always *easy*, but it can be done. We did it. We even did it without the anticipated catfight.

"We've created our own little *nirvana*. From the reactions we receive, it's obvious our relationship isn't typical—but we strongly believe it should be (and can be). There are obvious exceptions to every rule and we share our story to motivate and inspire divorced, young moms like us. You can bring peace and stability to your children's lives (and your own). We call this *enlightened living* and welcome you to read our blog, be encouraged by our own experience, and use our growing resources to create your own nirvana."

Their mantra: It's not about us— it's about the kids!

Another Perspective

My personal experience was quite different from Jill's and Shelley's. My ex-husband, Art, met his new significant other within a year of our divorce. She had experienced an unpleasant role as a stepmother in a prior marriage and was determined not to be involved with a stepchild in her new marriage.

For me, this worked out well. She never interfered or overstepped her role and was mostly absent when it came to discussions about my daughter. This left all of the interactions and co-parenting decisions between Art and me. In addition, she was always respectful to me and supportive of my role as Jessica's mom.

Her hands-off approach also worked because she worked when Jessica was at her father's house. Because of her schedule, Art's significant other had minimal interactions with my daughter. The time alone helped Jessica and her father build a very close relationship during their time together. Jessica often told me that she believed her relationship was closer with her father than a lot of her friends who lived with their dads seven days a week. I think this happened because they had one-on-one time together, as well as daily telephone conversations.

When Jessica was at Art's house, their time was theirs and theirs alone. Very rarely were there any other distractions. Unfortunately, Jessica and Art's significant other did not grow close or create a blended-family relationship.

This is a small price to pay, perhaps, for the greater benefit of the close father-daughter relationship that developed between Jessica and her dad, but it does have its downside. It is my true hope, and Jessica's as well, that sometime in the future the relationship will blossom and grow.

Overassertive Stepparents

Just to illustrate how different significant-other relationships can be, I want to tell you about Natalie, a young, energetic woman who came to see me shortly after I opened my family law practice.

Natalie was a force to be reckoned with—I could see that from the start. I recall our first consultation and thinking to myself, "Who is she talking about?" She spoke of the children as if they were hers, but also described in detail strong, aggravated feelings she had toward their mother. Her husband, a very busy businessman, had put her completely in charge of what went on in their household. He even sent her to my law office with a large retainer and a signed release to request modifications of the custody and parent plans for his children with his ex-wife. Her husband was only visible for court appearances and, even then, he always had Natalie by his side.

The case went on for well over a year. It shouldn't have been a surprise to me when the court-appointed mediator made a recommendation that Natalie, the stepmother, reduce her involvement with the children. The court-ordered recommendation described Natalie's relationship as overreaching, overbearing, and inappropriate.

As you can imagine, Natalie was very upset with me. How, she wondered, could I allow the court mediator to make such derogatory statements about her? The problem was that the mediator's statements were true. That was a lesson I'll never forget.

The bottom line is that the danger of over-assertive step-parenting is real. How do you know when a stepparent's involvement is too much or too little? You look for what works in your blended family—what feels right and where the balance is in your unique family situation.

The Nirvana Mommas have learned to co-parent in a partnership-like manner that is highly unusual, and for many, their relationship might be too unusual to use as a model of getting along. In contrast, my experience with my daughter's stepmother might be too minimal for the needs of many families.

The ultimate decision of how to blend a family with significant others should be determined between the family members, taking into account what is most comfortable and feels the most natural to everyone involved. Building blended families is complex. No one said it would be easy. But being respectful of the children, your co-parent, and the new significant other is key to making it all work.

~ EXERCISES ~

Your Family's Special Challenges
What are the special challenges you or your family face?

_____

_____

_____

_____

Thinking back to Week 4 where you learned to set long- and short-term goals, write down three small steps you can take to begin to resolve the special challenges you or your family face.

_____

_____

_____

_____

REVIEW OF WEEK 8

- Long-distance parents can stay in touch using technology, including cell phones with unlimited long distance for children and parents, instant messaging, and "webcams" that allow computer users to see each other while they talk.
- Long-distance parents can make their visiting children feel more comfortable by:
  - o Decorating the children's spaces together.
  - o Creating a Lego city that's always growing.
  - o Creating shared traditions, such as eating at a certain diner.
- Parallel parenting:
  - o Is an option for parents who are not able to parent collaboratively.
  - o Requires both parents to follow a very specific written parenting plan.
  - o Is not appropriate in cases involving mental illness, abuse, serious addictions, or a complete lack of parenting skills.
- In parallel parenting, parents work *separately* in the best interests of their children.

- In parallel parenting, do not discuss minor issues related to your children, tell the other parent how to parent, or bicker over things that have led to conflict in the past.
- Secondhand smoke can contribute to ear infections, bronchitis, asthma, and long-term poor health in children. It is also more harmful to infants and children than to adults.
- Secondhand smoke increases the risk of babies dying from Sudden Infant Death Syndrome (SIDS).
- Insist that no one smoke around your children.
- Addiction is the compulsive need for and use of a habit-forming substance.
- Addiction problems can strip people of their natural parenting instincts.
- A parent suffering from addiction needs to trust that there is hope for recovery.
- If domestic violence could occur during your breakup, it's important to have a safety plan.
- Parents should date new significant others when the children are not around.

WEEK 8 ACTION ITEMS

- Complete the exercises in Week 8.
- Journal about a special challenge you have overcome in your life.
- Review the goals you established in Week 4. Journal about your progress and the steps you plan to take to achieve your goals.

YOU CAN DO IT!

"You can't expect to hit the jackpot if you won't put a few nickels into the machine."
~ Flip Wilson, comedian

Back in the Introduction, I congratulated you for taking the first step toward becoming the best parent possible during the divorce process. You had 8 weeks of work ahead of you, but you took that first step—and then another and another. Congratulations again! You made it to the end.

During your 8-week journey, you learned a lot and I hope you have a feeling of accomplishment about the new skills you've acquired.

It's important to take stock of what you've learned, so take a moment to reflect on the past 8 weeks.

~ EXERCISE ~

What You Learned

What was the most important thing you learned that will result in a positive change in your co-parenting partnership?

_____

_____

_____

_____

_____

What did you learn that will result in something positive for yourself?

_____

_____

_____

_____

_____

What did you learn that will result in something positive for your child?

_____

_____

_____

_____

_____

Additionally, you learned that:

- The parent-child relationship is one of the most important bonds you'll ever have, so making wise decisions regarding parenting is critical for you and your children.
- Co-parenting starts with transforming your previous relationship into a businesslike parenting partnership.
- Letting go of the past helps you heal and move forward.
- Setting goals keeps life from just happening to you.
- Resolving conflict with your co-parent is important because exposure to parental conflict hurts children.
- One parenting style is not better than another style. They are just different.
- Managing your emotions can help you make decisions from a place of wisdom rather than from fear and anger.
- Co-parents need to communicate regularly to discuss their children's needs and progress.
- Children grow and change and these changes should be taken into account when designing or updating your parenting plan.
- Children need both parents.

You also gained some new parenting tools to help you be a more effective parent. Maybe you've even had a chance to put a few of these new skills to the test.

Now it's time to go out into the world and use your newly acquired knowledge and skills to be the best co-parent possible for your children. Change, of course, takes patience and practice. Don't expect to be transformed overnight. Practicing these principles will improve your relationship with your co-parent over time and make you a better parent to your children. Be patient. Keep moving forward.

You Can Do It! Action Items
- Complete the exercises in this section.
- Journal about steps you will take to maintain or improve the collaborative co-parenting skills you learned in this course.

Class Certification

There's an online review and test you can take to certify that you've taken a co-parenting course. The review course can be accessed at **www.CollaborativeCoparenting.com.**

The questions on the online test are right out of the material in this book. The test was designed both for parents who sign up for the online course *and* for parents who read the book. Feel free to refer to the book's review sections to answer the questions. I want you to be successful!

Additional Resources

When you go to the website (**www.CollaborativeCoparenting.com**), you'll find more information on co-parenting and links to other resources on subjects covered in this book. I believe that the more you know about co-parenting and parenting in general, the better equipped you'll be to be the best parent and person possible.

> *"Edison failed 10,000 times before he made the electric light. Do not be discouraged if you fail a few times."*
> *~ Napoleon Hill, self-help author*

Forever Parenting Partners

As you move forward into your new collaborative co-parenting partnership, some days will feel like you've taken two steps forward and others will feel like you're taking one step back. That's true of both your co-parenting partnership and life.

Just keep your forward momentum going and over time you will see progress and positive change. I have seen so many co-parents improve the lives of their children using the skills taught in this book that I know you can do it too.

Now that you've finished, I want you to sit back, close your eyes, breathe deeply, and think about the personal attitude required behind all the skills taught in this book. Really living these skills requires that you look at divorce differently and build a new kind of relationship with your co-parent that takes into account that you will always be parents together.

You may not be married anymore, but you will both always be your children's parents. This is a message your children need to know. Giving your children the gift of seeing their parents collaborate teaches them that people can forgive and treat each other with respect. I wish you the best as you move forward in your collaborative co-parenting partnership.

MORE PRAISE FOR *8 WEEKS TO COLLABORATIVE CO-PARENTING FOR DIVORCING PARENTS*

"Carol has transcended the co-parenting programs that are available at this time by asking parents to move to a peaceful place before approaching parenting issues with the other parent. What she asks and encourages parents to do is become better people. She speaks from both personal and professional experience in a manner that inspires parents to think beyond their feelings. Committing to this program, parents can find newfound power to turn a negative situation into a new way of being."
~Carol Fox, Licensed Marriage Family Therapist, Superior Court Private Mediator and Evaluator

"I am finding this book to be fun to read and worth its weight in gold; it is much more than another co-parenting book. It is very well organized and thought out, and reflects a deep understanding of the complex issues at play in this kind of elemental conflict. I think parents will find that it is a useful guide to improving not only their co-parenting, but their

whole post-divorce life, and what could be better for their kids than that?"
~Jack Love, Licensed Marriage Family Therapist, Co-Parent Counselor, Court Custody Mediator and Evaluator, Divorce Coach, and Child Specialist

"Instead of going to court and letting a judge make life-changing decisions for your family, read *8 Weeks to Collaborative Co-Parenting For Divorcing Parents*. It provides clear, practical advice for resolving conflict, communicating with your ex-spouse, and protecting your children's interests. This book will help families move past the pain of divorce and toward a new life."
~Alicia Santos-Coy, Licensed Marriage Family Therapist, Court Mediator

"*Collaborative Co-Parenting* is a must read for any divorcing couple with children. In clear language, Carol Delzer describes practical steps parents can take to continue to work together in the interests of their children. She offers guidelines on how to constructively problem-solve, and not let conflict derail the process. She helps parents keep the interests of their children paramount. Many children will benefit from this book."
~John H. O'Neal, M.D., Psychiatry, Author *Child and Adolescent Clinical Psychopharmacology Made Simple*

"Carol offers divorcing couples an authentic approach to deal with heartache while creating a co-parenting program that protects children from the ravages of divorce."
~Linda Tell, RN, Marriage Family Therapist, Superior Court Mediator, Collaborative Divorce Coach, and Child Specialist

"I have been in family law for the last twenty years, serving as a mediator, evaluator and special master. I am very impressed

by the advice and clinical direction Carol offers. If parents adopt the principles advocated by the author, they will be able to keep their children out of the divorce conflict. I wholeheartedly recommend this book to anyone in family court."
~ Thomas Russell, Licensed Clinical Social Worker, Court Mediator, Special Master

"As an experienced family law attorney and trained mediator and collaborative professional, I believe this book can be a valuable tool for all parents going through a divorce and an excellent guide on how parents can preserve their relationships with their children and develop a structure for their future relationship. This book will also provide insight to attorneys, mediators, religious leaders, therapists, and other professionals who work with divorcing families to effectively help parents and their children through their troubling times."
~Mark Johannessen, Collaborative Attorney, CPA

"This book includes practical co-parenting tools and also addresses the emotions that often get in the way of divorcing partners being good parents. It will be extraordinarily useful to divorcing parents, to the benefit of children 'caught in the middle.' The last three chapters are invaluable and bring a sharp focus to the actual parenting tools and strategies that will help resolve conflicts, gain your children's trust, and lay the foundation for long-term success. Carol Delzer's book fills a niche in the body of knowledge on cooperative divorce and co-parenting that has been desperately needed. I highly recommend it."
~Deni Deutsch Marshall, Licensed Clinical Social Worker, Collaborative Divorce Coach, and Child Specialist

"An excellent and very practical book for parents who are divorced. This book captures the importance of communication and co-parenting. This book is easy to read, well organized,

and provides parents with a wide range of information regarding co-parenting. The step-by-step approach to co-parenting and effective communication will make you a better parent."
~Penny R. Hancock, Marriage Family Therapist, Private Court Mediator and Evaluator, Child Specialist, and Divorce Coach

"Collaborative co-parenting is the primary vital ingredient in helping your children heal and have successful, loving lives. In my role as a mediator and custody evaluator, the children I interview tell me they don't care who wins, they just want their parents to please stop fighting."
~Timothy B. Rood, Licensed Marriage Family Therapist, Court Mediator and Evaluator—California Superior Court, Child Specialist, and Divorce Coach

"This book is terrific—very uplifting. It will be very, very helpful to people going through a divorce. The book normalizes divorce and gives very good guidelines to navigate that journey successfully."
~Elly McGeary Fossum, Licensed Marriage Family Therapist, Collaborative Divorce Coach, and Child Specialist

"Children of divorce have a tough enough time dealing with their parents' fallout without having to also deal with their parents' negative emotions. *8 Weeks to Collaborative Co-Parenting for Divorcing Parents* will help parents realize how their actions impact their children while providing tips on changing those actions into something more positive. All newly single parents will benefit from this book and learn how to better work together for the sake of their children."
~Kelly K. Payne, Family Law Attorney

"*8 Weeks to Collaborative Co-Parenting for Divorcing Parents* is a pathway for couples to continue the family through a divorce."
Marvin Todd, Ph.D., Licensed Clinical Social Worker, Author *Linked for Life: How Our Siblings Affect Our Lives*

"Carol has brought together important concepts for parents who are raising children in two homes. She has combined the personal experience of shared parenting, the legal experience of being an attorney working with many families, and the healing environment of a person trained in Marriage and Family Counseling. I strongly recommend *8 Weeks to Collaborative Co-Parenting For Divorcing Parents*."
~Frank Leek, Ph.D., Developer and Author of the *Shared Parenting Support Program*

"I encourage all parents who are experiencing the end of their relationship to commit to Carol Delzer's *8 Weeks to Collaborative Co-Parenting for Divorcing Parents*. Your children will always be the most precious parts of your entire life experience, to be cherished, nourished with love, and protected. The impact of parental separation is profound, requiring a commitment to your children that can be learned, developed, and shared. This hopefully will start at the beginning of your relationship difficulties. You need the benefit of gifted and experienced hands to help you and the other parent to effectively co-parent, wherever you are in starting your life apart from the other parent. As a Certified Family Law Specialist, California State Bar Board of Specialization since 1980, and practicing family law attorney for more than thirty-seven years, I am delighted to read Carol's journey. Congratulations to you for committing to this journey, and upon finishing it you will embrace a new and more meaningful life as a better parent."
~Vince Jacobs, Attorney, Certified Family Law Specialist

"Carol Delzer, an experienced family law attorney, has years of experience helping families cope with divorce prior to the divorce and post divorce. She is an accomplished author of articles and books written about divorce, specifically parenting children and coping strategies. *8 Weeks to Collaborative Co-Parenting for Divorcing Parents* is a book that should be on every bookshelf for professionals as well as for families because Carol has put her energy and professional knowledge into helping families cope with the challenge of raising children in two separate homes by giving them practical advice and strategies for parenting and conflict resolution."
~Mary Ann Frank, Ph.D., Licensed Marriage Family Therapist

"This guide should aid any parent seeking how best to approach what schedule will best serve their children as the parents transition into separate households."
~Paul Brimberry, Collaborative Attorney, Certified Family Law Specialist, Children's Counsel